ROOMIES

Ed –
All my best

[signature]

DON FARMER / SKIP CARAY

ROOMiES

TALES FROM THE

WORLDS OF TV NEWS

AND SPORTS

LONGSTREET PRESS
Atlanta, Georgia

Published by LONGSTREET PRESS, INC.,
a subsidiary of Cox Newspapers,
a division of Cox Enterprises, Inc.
2140 Newmarket Parkway
Suite 118
Marietta, Georgia 30067

Printed in the United States of America

1st printing, 1994

Library of Congress Catalog Number 94-77588

ISBN: 1-56352-176-8

This book was printed by Maple-Vail Book Manufacturing Group, York, PA.

Jacket and book design by Laura McDonald

TABLE of CONTENTS

To my mother, Doris Farmer, who didn't live
to see *Roomies* published, but who endured countless tellings
of my stories with encouragement and support.
— *Don Farmer*

To my family — you're the best.
— *Skip Caray*

FOREWORD

When the phone rang I had to decide which hand I would take off the rail on my treadmill to answer it. I was in my thirty-fourth minute on the machine and my breath was labored.

Having "Geraldo" on the TV in the exercise room didn't help. I had wasted some valuable treadmill breath yelling back at the screen. It's easy to get emotional when Geraldo presents his freak of the day. This time it was a Nazi sword swallower who claimed that Betty Crocker was his love slave. Betty was a no-show and Geraldo was cranky.

So when I answered the phone, I was panting. And what I heard coming back at me was more panting.

"Hey Roomie . . . pant . . . pant . . . huff . . . huff . . . what are you doing?"

It was Skip, and the shortness of breath was his, not an echo of mine.

"I'm on the treadmill," I said in a burst of breath, trying to sound as far from my target heart rate as possible.

"Stairmaster here," he gasped.

We both started laughing. We had each caught the other doing something we hated at the moment in hopes that it would give us more years of life to do the things we love. Our mutual huffing and puffing also brought home the realization that our thirty-six years of friendship had come full circle.

We began in a fraternity house at the University of Missouri, abusing our bodies with beer and fried things and 4:00 a.m.

omelets and grain alcohol and cigarettes and more beer. We had learned the secret handshake of the Phi Gamma Delta fraternity and had worn the silly secret robes and had survived all that to graduate from the U. of Mo. School of Journalism.

Now, thirty-six years after we had kicked each other's dirty socks under the beds in that cramped fraternity-house dorm room, we were in the same town — Atlanta — and in the same business — broadcasting. And on this November morning, as we huffed and puffed through a truly mobile phone conversation, we were both pumping our legs on expensive machinery in order to deny that time and gravity had been at war with us for the past three and a half decades.

It seemed such a short time ago that we more or less broke into radio together at the small AM station in Columbia, Missouri. We were better than most of our peers at that place and time, but we were not nearly as good as we hoped we were.

It seemed such a short time ago that we got drunk in a bar in St. Louis and offered a recording contract to the lounge trio. We had no record company of course; we were young and poor and full of ourselves, but the bass player didn't know that, and the drummer and the clarinet guy went along with the idea because we bought them sixty-four drinks.

We were just starting out in life and thought that hiring a trio would be a great way to break in. We make more sense and drink a lot less now.

But once in awhile, I wonder what happened to that bass player. His name was Percy James the Third, and I'll bet he never tortured himself on a treadmill.

— DON FARMER

So there we were, my old college roommate and I, trying to carry on a phone conversation — he huffing away on his treadmill, me puffing away on my Stairmaster — two old farts who first met in 1957 at the University of Missouri when I was a freshman and he a sophomore. Somehow we wound up together in the same city 800 miles from where we first met.

Farmer has made it big in the news business. He's been a foreign correspondent for ABC; he, along with his beautiful wife Chris Curle, helped Ted Turner get CNN off the ground; and, for the past several years, he has anchored the six and eleven o'clock news broadcasts for Atlanta's leading news station, WSB.

I, on the other hand, have labored in the sports broadcast vineyard, doing pro basketball, football, and baseball primarily in Atlanta and primarily for Turner's WTBS and TNT.

Our labored discussion while we exercised centered around a football game we were all attending and about where to go for dinner and drinks afterward. We went to the game, had the drinks and the dinner, and laughed about our panting phone chat. To us it seems like only yesterday that we were college kids. Now we try to prolong our lives with mechanical torture devices.

We began to reflect during dinner that night on where the time had gone for both of us and how much fun we'd had and how many strange things had happened to us in our respective careers in front of the television camera.

Ordinarily, the only people who write books about television are the producers, because they don't have anything else to do. They write about how they "made" this announcer or that one. This book is different; it certainly isn't intended to be a heavy treatise.

Life in television is sort of high risk. Unlike writers, you're often up there live — without a net, as they say — and, like anything else where human beings are concerned, live television prompts big-time mistakes. This book is about some of what we hope are the funnier of those errors and some of the other strange and wacky things that have happened to us in our trips throughout the country and the world. In many cases the names have been changed to protect the guilty.

The stories are true — at least true enough — and we hope that you'll enjoy them. In fact, we hope you'll enjoy them so much so that we can retire and not worry about those few poor souls who will be unhappy with these pages. Mostly they will be management types. But then, you already knew that, didn't you.

To every announcer who's screwed it up live — and that's all of us — we dedicate this book.

— SKIP CARAY

ROOMiES

Ah, YOUTH!

GOOD
NIGHT,
SKIP

The two things I wanted most as a kid were to have a dog and to be Skip Caray. Understand, I didn't want to be *like* Skip. I wanted to *be* him. I had never met him, of course, but as a grade schooler who worshipped the St. Louis Cardinals, I knew all about Skip.

His famous father, Harry Caray, was the voice of the Cardinals on radio in those days, and I hung on Harry's every word as I followed my team.

I already was blessed by the fact that Enos Slaughter, the legendary Cardinals outfielder, lived in the same town as I did — Ferguson, in north St. Louis County. (A few years ago, I drove my wife by the house where Enos Slaughter lived when I was a kid. It was the Ferguson equivalent of the Baseball Hall of Fame. She was politely reverent.)

So night after night in those summers of my youth, I would go to bed listening to the Cardinals games on the radio. Every night at nine o'clock, Harry Caray would be saying something memorable, such as, "Heerrre's the stretch, the pitch, STRIKE TWO!!!" and I would say it too, exactly the way he did, only very softly so my mom would not hear and come upstairs and take away the radio under the covers.

I could imitate Harry pretty well because I wanted to be like him when I grew up. I wanted to be *like* Harry, but I wanted to *be* Skip.

But back to nine o'clock. Every night at nine, Harry would pause from the game call for a moment and say, "Good night, Skip; go to bed now, son."

Damn that kid, I thought, the little punk, getting his name on the radio every night. Damn damn damn . . . how come this kid gets to be famous, just because his dad is a radio announcer?

I used to fantasize that Skip had no arms and would never be able to throw a baseball, while I, the broadcast unknown that I was, played first base on my little league team and batted third!

See, life could be the great evener. But I knew that Skip probably did have arms and probably did play ball and probably was the hero on his little league team because his dad was Harry Caray.

I even made up a scenario once that turned the tables. Skip wanted to be a chemist when he grew up, but had no connections in that profession. I, however, was a true insider because my dad was a chemist and had to measure stuff for medicine that could make people well, so Skip just envied the hell out of me. At least that's how I imagined it.

When I got to know Skip in college, I was disappointed to know that being a chemist never entered his mind. He also had arms that worked well enough, which blew another of my fantasies to hell.

I also found out, however, how he felt about his dad telling him on the radio every night to go to bed.

HA! He hated it.

FOND

MEMORIES

A favorite story from my college days concerns a kid who finally, in his last semester of journalism school, got a chance to broadcast the 11:55 p.m. news from that wonderful old newsroom of the *Columbia Tribune*. The kid was terrible, but he worked for nothing. He thought he was a good deal better than he was and even began clearing his throat before every pronouncement in class. Soon, on chilly spring days, he took to wearing a scarf to protect his vocal chords. All this for a lousy five-minute newscast heard by just about nobody. I ran into him on campus one day and he complained long and hard about how his throat was hurting him. I told him I'd stay and do his show if it really bothered him, but the thought of missing a chance to be on the air was too much for him. He said thanks, but no thanks.

I went about my business and rushed off to meet a lovely young lady of great beauty, warmth, and wit and no discernible virtue. She was wonderful, and I was a normal twenty-year-old horny college student. By 11:55 said young lady and I were in the throes of passion in the backseat of my car in an area of Columbia known as Hinkson Creek. Rumor had it that if you threw a rock into Hinkson Creek it would bounce back to you because of all the prophylactics in its channel. Be that as it may, Sinatra was blaring on KFRU, and magic was in the air as the time approached 11:55. They threw it to the news. I could have cared less. But instead of the news we were treated to the sounds of a tape being played at the wrong speed and the hoarse voice of our news announcer exclaiming, "OHHH SHIT!"

The idiot had taped the news to make sure he sounded alright. We'll never know if he did or not, because his career on the air came to a close and I suffered for the first time from coitus-interruptus — which is what happens when you begin laughing hysterically during sex. The young lady was not amused, but, being a good sport, came with me to the radio station where we found the disc jockey laughing as hard as I was. I did the news between giggles, and the day was saved.

■ ■ ■

I was fortunate as a youngster to get a chance to work at what I feel was then the greatest radio station in the country. KMOX was the voice of St. Louis, and Robert Hyland, who ran the place for more than a quarter of a century, was the fairest and the most demanding boss I've ever had. He arrived at work at five in the morning and stayed til seven or eight o'clock each night. That was six days a week. On Sundays he only worked eight hours or so. We were doing talk radio before it came into vogue; the program was called "At Your Service."

Our job was made immensely difficult by the unions. KMOX was a CBS-owned and -operated station in those days, and you not only had the brotherhood of electrical workers (radio engineers) to contend with but also the union. Radio had pretty much put an end to the Big Band era, so to get our program on the air we had an announcer on one side of the glass and a producer on the other (me at times), as well as an engineer who ran the controls, and an out-of-work musician who rolled the platters on which, in those days, the commercials were stored. The chance for screw-ups was enhanced by the power of five, since five guys are bound to screw up what one or two could handle much more easily. The business hasn't changed much in that regard.

At KMOX I may have been the man who inadvertently invented the seven-second delay, which is now in use to keep obscene
callers off the air. What you hear on the air is delayed on tape by
seven seconds so the profanities
can be erased. One portion of "At
Your Service" was hosted by
the sports editor of the then *St.
Louis Globe-Democrat* — a delightful man named Bob Burnes.
Each Thursday night his guest
was the outdoor editor of his
paper, a gent named George
Carson who — for an hour —
would tell those interested where
the best places to fish were and
where the Bambi-murderers
would have the best chance of
finding their prey. I guess it
was interesting to people who
hunt and fish, but to people
like the producer of the program (me) it was pretty deadly
stuff. Still I faithfully screened
the calls and tried to get rid of
the wackos before they hit the
air. One fine Thursday it went
something like this:

BURNES: "Your question or
comment please?"

CALLER: "I have a request
for George Carson."

*Skip, (top) a freshman, and Don, a
sophomore, are Phi Gamma Delta fraternity brothers at the University of
Missouri in 1958.*

BURNES: "What is your
request?"

CALLER: "I request you all
go f--k yourselves."

We went to seven-second delay the next day, and it's been a
staple of the talk radio business ever since.

MONEY MATTERS (PUN INTENDED)

The pursuit of girls to date and money to spend on those dates consumed a lot of my time in college. I was not particularly good at acquiring either, but I worked hard at it.

One day in the fall of 1959, my junior year, Skip offered me a job.

"My dad's doing the Mizzou game this weekend, and he needs a spotter. It pays twenty dollars," he said.

"I'll do it," I answered, and he told me to be at the stadium an hour before the game.

What a deal — twenty dollars for sitting in the radio booth with Harry Caray and watching the Missouri Tigers' football game. Not only would I be making about five dollars an hour, but I could probably put it on my job resume with Harry Caray's name in big letters.

Then it dawned on me that I had no idea what a spotter was or what a spotter did in a broadcast booth.

I could ask Skip, but that might scare him into withdrawing the offer. So I asked another of my fraternity brothers who was a football fanatic.

"A spotter? Jeez, that's no sweat," he said. "You just gotta watch the play and tell the announcer who did what — like, who carried the ball and who tackled him or whatever."

Armed with that knowledge, I showed up at the press entrance to the stadium that Saturday afternoon. It was an hour before kickoff, but Harry Caray already was in the booth, poring over game notes put out by both teams. He knew the Tigers inside out and was now learning the other team's players by position and number.

"Hey, kid, nice to see ya," Harry said as he handed me a program. "You know the drill, right?"

"Well, sure, but I want to brush up, too," I said.

Harry's producer showed me a large square board, divided into smaller squares. In each square was a player's name and number and position — the Tigers on the left, the other Big Eight team on the right. It became clear very quickly that my job was to point to the correct players on the board, first the ball carrier or

pass receiver, then the tackler or tacklers on the play, and then anyone else who might be involved.

That way, Harry could describe the play as he glanced down at
my nimble fingers pointing to the key players.

He had done it a thousand times, but this day was different. He
never before had worked with a spotter who didn't know anything about football, didn't know the players' positions or numbers,
and had never seen a spotter's board before.

What unfolded from the opening kickoff was a nightmarish
blur of incompetence. Mine.

I could not keep up.

First of all, I had trouble seeing the players' numbers on the plays
because they kept crashing into each other and falling down in heaps.
I had the quarterback figured out by about the second series of
downs, but all the other guys looked more or less alike to me.

Luckily, the Missouri team had black helmets with gold trim, and
the other guys had on red and white, so I usually could tell which team
any given guy was on. But in one of those pile-on heaps, who knew?

Harry was a trooper, slurring over the tacklers' names whenever possible — or necessary, since he wasn't getting much help
from the spotter's board or from me, the spotter.

My hands would be in the air, shoulders in shrug mode, face
drained, all of which screamed silently to Harry and his team, "I
have no idea what I'm doing, can't you see that?"

During the first commercial break, Harry whispered something
to his producer. When play resumed, the producer kept leaning over
my shoulder. For a while, he tried to guide my hand to point to the
correct places on the board. But he gave that up after I had the defensive left tackle intercepting a 45-yard pass, which in reality had been
caught by an offensive tight end.

"Let me show you," he seethed, and sat down in my place as I
jumped up and out of his way. The producer then did the spotting
for Harry until half time.

At that point, Mr. Caray took off his headphones, turned to me
and said, "Don, I don't think you're up to it today, OK?"

"I'm really sorry, Mr. Caray, but I just can't seem to keep up with
you."

"I'm not setting the pace, son," he said, his voice calmer now. "The game does that. I just keep up, or try to, and it's a whole lot tougher to do that when my spotter is somewhere earlier in the game — no offense of course."

I suggested that maybe I should not continue in the second half.

"Well, that's up to you," Harry said.

"No, I think you've had enough for one day," chimed in the producer. He was right, of course.

Harry Caray always will be one of my heroes, because he let me down easy and paid me the twenty dollars anyway.

I had a date that night and spent it all on the evening. She asked me about my afternoon with Harry Caray. I told her it was cool, but that I probably wouldn't want to do it again.

When I saw Skip Sunday at dinner in the fraternity house, he asked me with a straight face how the "spotting" went.

"OK, but it was tougher than I thought," I said.

He smiled and said, "Great, can I borrow twenty dollars?"

■ ■ ■

That's the news up to the minute. Next here on KFRU — 'Sports Final with Skip Caray.'"

That was me talking on a Friday night in the fall of 1959, in the news booth, a small, soundproof, glass-enclosed room in the newsroom of the Columbia, Missouri, *Daily Tribune.*

I was a senior in the Journalism School at the U. of Missouri and had landed a coveted job doing the 10:00 p.m. newscast on the station owned by the newspaper. I was getting paid $1 per hour.

Skip was a junior and already had the job of doing the 10:10 sports, a ten-minute wrap of sports news and scores.

One night, another student and I were trying to think of a way to break him up while he was on the air.

He was, after all, the son of the famous Harry Caray, born to the business, so to speak. So there was a spark of envy once in awhile from the rest of us, whose dads were chemists or carpenters or contract killers or something other than famous sportscasters.

As we watched Skip doing the sports in the same glass booth I had just vacated, we considered the possibilities, wanting to make sure that the trick would not be lethal . . . to us.

We discarded the hackneyed radio tricks, such as setting fire to his script or cutting it in half with long-bladed copy shears as he was reading on the air. He was a pro, after all; he could deal with the usual pranks.

My friend Jim finally had a thought. It was sweet. It was perfect.

"Fantastic. Tomorrow night, we'll do it. Gimme your ten bucks and I'll arrange it," I said.

I knew what glee felt like, anticipating Skip's first major on-air screw-up, at least the first one arranged by me, his roomie.

MY NEWSCAST THAT FRIDAY NIGHT was routine, but I was upbeat, full of energy, excited. My voice was saying something about a bond issue or a pothole, but my mind was on what was going to happen to Skip in just a few minutes.

"Hello again, everybody; this is Skip Caray," he said, starting "Sports Final" that Friday night.

Football was his number-one story. The Mizzou Tigers were playing a home game the next day, and he went into some detail about the Tigers' chances.

I went to the front door of the newsroom and looked outside. There she was, sitting in her car at the curb. She was a part-time student and part-time party girl.

"Hi, come on in," I said. She got out of the car, wearing a fur coat, roughly knee-length, as promised, and buttoned up with the collar pulled together at her neck.

As she came inside, I slipped two $10 bills into the pocket of her coat.

"You'll be out of here in five minutes. Just go to that door on the side of the news booth, open it, step in and sit on Skip's lap."

I told her not to say a word, whispered a final instruction, and stepped away. Skip didn't even look up through the glass as he read his sports copy.

Just as he began reading about the other Big Eight conference games scheduled for the next day, the girl (let's call her Tanya) opened the booth door and plopped down on Skip's lap.

He tried to push her off but couldn't get any leverage. He was, after all, reading football news at that moment, on a live radio show.

He offered a killer look through the glass and saw us bent over with laughter. I turned up the monitor outside the booth so we could hear what I expected to be Skip cursing or hollering or both.

But he kept reading — Kansas State this or that, Oklahoma Sooners on a roll, whatever — as Tanya ran her fingers over Skip's hair and down the back of his neck.

"The Cornhuskers are (slight pause as he swatted her hand away), um, up against it tomorrow in Lincoln (another pause to glare at me) against Oklahoma State . . ."

Then Tanya opened the coat buttons and let the fur slide onto Skip's lap. She was naked and very cool about it, but Skip started to sweat. He looked, briefly, at her body, then back at his copy, his hands starting to shake.

"At the fieldhouse today, the basketball Tigers . . ." His voice faded a bit as Tanya squirmed. He raised a fist at me through the glass, then shoved Tanya to her right.

She smiled silently and stood up. The fur coat remained on Skip's lap. She blew him a kiss and stepped out of the booth. Then, remembering that the coat and the cash were still in there with Skip, she reached back in, yanked the coat off his lap and closed the door.

He forgave me, in a month or so. I assumed all that time that he was plotting revenge, but it never happened, unless you count his total success in the sports broadcasting business. And that surely is the best revenge.

GETTING STARTED

THE BIG

TIME

ABC News was young, in third place, and on a low budget when I got a job there in 1965. Nevertheless, getting hired there — both the process and the event — was a dream come true. I was based in New York; I was a network correspondent at age twenty-six, one of the youngest ever hired.

I knew I was plenty lucky on the day I went to the office of Elmer Lower for an interview. Mr. Lower, then the president of ABC News, is a widely respected veteran of TV news. To be in his office, having him offer me a job, was a momentous experience. What I remember most, however, was the image on the TV set across from Elmer Lower's desk.

It was a young, handsome guy, sitting on a news set, reading to the camera. He would start, read, stop, turn to the side, then back to the camera, and so on.

"Who's that?" I asked Mr. Lower.

"Oh, you may be working with him soon. I think we're gonna hire him as our new anchorman. He does well in Canada."

It was Peter Jennings, auditioning for the anchor job at ABC News.

ON APRIL 4, 1965, MY FIRST REAL day at work, Mr. Lower had his assistant show me to the newsroom, the nerve center of the ABC network news department, the hub of that electronic universe, the pulse of the nation, all that.

What it was was a series of small, windowless rooms in the basement of an ABC building at 7 West 66th Street in New York. The correspondents' room was a drab place, with two ugly metal desks that looked like they were probably military surplus. ABC had eight correspondents based in New York at that time: Barrie Dunsmore (also a new hire), Jim Burnes, Bernie Eisman, Mal Goode, Don Goddard, John McBain, a couple of others, and me, all reporting each morning to the bottom of the building, all competing for those two desks.

I hardly ever got one, because I lived in Westchester County and took the New Haven commuter train to work. It was very hard for me to get to work ahead of the guys who lived in Manhattan. The first two correspondents in the office every day got the two desks.

Each desk had a manual typewriter on it. Two desks, two typewriters, eight reporters.

Occasionally we would adjust our milling around so that one guy could use the typewriter on one side of the desk top, while another reporter could use the regular desk space. We would pass the phone back and forth as needed.

Once in awhile we would wander down the dingy hall and perch on the corner of Walter Porges' workplace — the news assignment desk. Walter is a quiet man, talented in a way almost too classy for TV news. He indulged us rookies lounging on his turf. The nastiest typical-news-editor-type thing Walter ever said to us was, "Guys, get your butts off the desk; you're sitting on tomorrow's coverage plans for the whole country."

One of the correspondents who seemed to be among the most friendly was a veteran, a native New Yorker with several years at ABC News. He seemed so self-assured, so at ease, that when he gave advice, I usually listened. One day, I was standing at the corner of one of the two reporters' desks, leaning over, trying to fill out an expense account form.

That worldly correspondent walked over, saw the form, saw my expenses — taxi, phones, maybe a lunch with some newsmaker — and whispered, "I can help you."

"What?"

"I can help you with that, make you some extra money," he said.

The conversation was interrupted by Walter Porges calling from the assignment desk. Within six hours, I was on a plane to Dixie.

ON MY FIFTH DAY AS A NETWORK correspondent, ABC sent me to Montgomery, Alabama, to cover civil rights demonstrations there. Four days later, I was off to Bogalusa, Louisiana, for more confrontations between blacks and the Ku Klux Klan, with the FBI more or less trying to keep the two sides apart.

It was my first lesson that "Yankee" reporters were not welcome in the white community. The FBI didn't give a damn about us either. Bogalusa was a tense, smelly town then — tense because of the racial strife and smelly because of the odiferous fumes from the local paper mill. To this day, I associate the smell of a paper mill with fear.

On April 16, blacks gathered at one end of Columbia Avenue for a march. Klan members milled around at the other end of the street. In the middle were a handful of FBI agents. The other reporters and I, with our camera crews, bunched near the FBI, waiting.

To our right, the black people began to move toward us. To our left, the KKK people, some in robes and pointy hats, also began to advance in our direction. Suddenly, without a word, the FBI agents jogged to their cars and drove away, leaving us in the middle of the street, demonstrators on one side, Klansmen on the other.

Don, shortly after being hired by ABC News in 1965.

We were in deep trouble, and the FBI could not have cared less.

My cameraman, Chuck Pharris, already was a veteran of the hazards of covering the civil rights movement. He walked slowly over, camera on his shoulder, not filming, and whispered, "Don, down here, when the FBI leaves, we leave."

I glanced up and down the street, scared and nervous but reluctant to miss a story.

"We all should go, right *now*," Chuck hissed, and we did. Like sandpipers leaving a beach in formation, the three network crews and reporters shuffled across Columbia Avenue and down a side-street. We still could see the demonstrators, but we were out of the line of fire.

The demonstrators stopped, sang, and chanted and retreated to a black church nearby. The Klansmen, confused by the blacks' departure, hollered and hooted and swore at us, then got bored and left. It was, as confrontations went in those days, a minor snapshot of bluff and bluster, not even a footnote in the history of the civil rights movement. But it was my first brush with the potential for violence that I would see realized, soon and often.

Through the next few years, I was lucky enough to be an eye-witness to the movement and to become an acquaintance of Dr. Martin Luther King, Jr. I saw him gain world fame. I saw his courage and his flaws, and I covered his assassination and the awful aftermath.

But that one hot, smelly, sweaty, frightful day in Bogalusa is burned into my memory. It was my introduction to the movement that changed the world.

A WEEK OR SO LATER, I WAS BACK in New York, competing for a desk, awaiting another exciting assignment. But the stories in town were pretty tame. One day I interviewed Adam Clayton Powell in Harlem. Another day I had to cover Armenian Martyrs Day, a march at the United Nations. The interest around the country in that event was underwhelming.

On a slow Saturday in April, I learned another lesson about working with camera crews. Some of them don't mind taking advantage of a rookie.

The weekend news wanted a short feature on daylight savings time at a clock shop in Greenwich Village. As we finished that sparkler and got back in the crew car, the radio crackled. The desk wanted us to rush to a student protest demonstration at Columbia University in upper Manhattan.

"Let's go," I said, trying to sound cool.

"Well, we really can't go up there yet," responded the cameraman, a guy about two years from retirement who had no interest in pushing his way into a bunch of angry college students.

"Why not?" I asked him.

"We have a rule here. You probably don't know about it yet, being new and all," he said. "Whenever we shoot a story, like the one here at the clock store, we have to take the film back to the studios and get it developed before we can go on to our next assignment."

"But this is a feature and the thing at Columbia is spot news,"

I responded, frustrated by the guy's obvious attempt to avoid the demonstration.

"Sorry, a rule's a rule," he said, starting the engine and driving north toward the ABC headquarters on the West side.

I thought about it for a minute and decided to take a chance: "Tell you what. Let's radio the office and let them decide, OK?"

He paused, made a left turn and headed toward Columbia University.

THE NEXT DAY, THE CORRESPONDENT who was so concerned about my expense accounts approached me again.

"Remember we talked about doing expenses?" he asked.

"I think I've got the hang of it," I said.

He shook his head, looked around the room and leaned closer.

"Tell you what — for ten percent of your profit, I can show you how to turn your expense account into a cash cow."

I demurred, embarrassed but curious.

"No sweat, just always bring your voucher to me before you turn it in. I'll give it a little creative editing, add a zero here and there, and we both win, OK?"

I didn't think much of that, but I told him I would think about it.

"Whatever," he said, with the confident look of a man who had successfully made the same offer to others.

IN

THE

MINORS

In 1962 I got a chance to broadcast minor league baseball in Tulsa, Oklahoma, for the Cardinals AA Texas League team, whose general manager was a delightful fellow named Hugh Finnerty. I was one of three announcers, along with veterans Mack Creager and Len Morton. In those days we used to broadcast the away games by means of wire re-creations. We would get a Western Union code that told us what was happening. "S1C" meant "strike one called." "B1OS" meant "ball one outside" and so on. All the rest we invented as we went along. It was the way my dad had done major league games some fifteen years before.

I ran into a little trouble my first night when the ticker sent me "FOG." I blithely announced that the game had been delayed by fog and was ready to roll some rain-delay music when my partners whispered to me that "FOG" meant "foul over grandstand." Thank God I got a little better as things went along.

OUR TEAM WAS THE TULSA OILERS, a pretty good farm team at that time. In fact, at one point in the season, the Oilers took a six-game winning streak on the road to El Paso. I was in the studio doing the wire re-creation. We would start our broadcast thirty minutes after the game began and try to time it to gradually catch up, so that by the ninth inning we were pitch for pitch with the telegraph wire and totally at the mercy of whomever the sender happened to be.

The Oilers were hooked up in a tie game as El Paso batted in the bottom of the ninth, and I was right with them. Jose Cardenal (later a major league star) was hitting for El Paso, and, according to the ticker, he homered to win the game. I said, "Here's the wind, the pitch . . . there's a drive to deep left. Jim Beauchamp looks up, but that ball is gone and the Oilers winning streak is history. Final score . . . El Paso 7, Tulsa 6. Totals and highlights in a moment." I was busy totaling things up in my scorebook when the machine began chattering again. I glanced up. It said: "CORRECTION . . . CORRECTION . . . Cardenal's ball ruled foul. Cardenal grounds out. Inning over." What to do? When in doubt, tell the truth. When we got back from the commercial, I explained what had happened, apologized, and went back to work.

The Oilers eventually won the game. I stopped and had a drink or two and headed for my tiny little studio apartment figuring I had done the very best I could. The next morning I arose and headed to the coffee shop down the block for my morning cup of java. I bought a paper, sat at the counter in the crowded diner, politely ordered my coffee and opened the paper, turning quickly to the sports page. Then I screamed, "JESUS CHRIST!" at the top of my lungs. The headline on the sports page read: OILERS STREAK ENDS ON LATE CARDENAL HOMER.

I had forgotten that the paper didn't send their writer on the road with the team either. He sat at the sports desk, listened to the game, then filed his story. When he heard the game end the first time he shut me off and began writing his story to beat his deadline. It took us a couple of weeks to get it all straightened out.

Incidentally, I never went back to the diner again. Too embarrassed.

I'VE STATED HOW IMPORTANT THE Western Union sender was to us announcers, hundreds of miles away from the game. Some of them were really great. Others less than that.

In one International League city there were two fellows who worked together on the games. We'll call them Hal and Elmer, even though those were not the fellows' real names. Hal and Elmer were not baseball fans at all. They were apparently very close friends, and both of them were more interested in beauty than they were in baseball. They would send things like, "Today's game is being played under a brilliant azure sky. And Johnny Doe is the batter. He has rippling biceps and a strong chin." Old Hal and Elmer had a helluva time, but it was a little rough on the other end of the wire. I hope they are alive and well and still dealing in rhapsody.

MINOR LEAGUE BASEBALL WAS A lot of fun, though. The players were dirt poor. So were the announcers. Nobody had an agent, and everybody seemed happier than they are today. Strange things happened in the minor leagues. In Atlanta I served as the team's public relations director for Bill McKechnie back in the early '60s and once joined in breaking up a fight between two of our Latin players. One of them had gotten hold of an ice pick and was trying to perforate the other for casting a voodoo curse on him. Fortunately, that kind of incident was rare.

Also in Atlanta, the Crackers used to play a game at the Federal Penitentiary against the prison team just before the season opened. One year I broadcast the game with a delightful convict on the prison radio station. Making conversation, I asked the guy, "What are you in for?" He smiled, shrugged, and said, "I smoked my wife. But it's no big deal." Never was I so happy for a game to end.

Jack McKeon, our manager that year, arranged for one of our players — Chuck Weatherspoon — to be detained by the prison authorities as we headed for the bus that would take us back to freedom. I don't know what had gone on in Spoon's past, but he was one terrified guy until he was told that it was a joke.

OFTEN IN THE MINOR LEAGUES THE best team would try to dump games late in the year. It was no nefarious plot involving gamblers. Instead, it was a chance for the best players to get called to the major leagues rather than picking up a couple of hundred dollars for a minor league playoff share. Some of the worst throws and worst swings I've ever seen came from the best players on certain minor league teams. Remember . . . the names have been deleted to protect the guilty.

SOUTHERN
SCENES

Working in the Southern Bureau (Atlanta) for ABC News was a trip, literally. As bureau chief and correspondent, I was away from home most of the time during the turbulent days of the civil rights movement in the mid- and late sixties.

I worked with camera crews from various ABC News bureaus, plus some freelancers, as I bolted around the South, covering Dr. King and his movement, running to keep up with Charles Evers in Mississippi, running to keep away from state troopers' tear gas in towns from South Georgia to New Orleans.

One of our most frequent stops was Jackson, Mississippi. We would arrive on a Delta flight with about fourteen metal travel cases full of camera equipment. "We" included a cameraman, a soundman, a lightman, and me, the correspondent.

First stop in the Jackson airport was a rent-a-car counter to find the car with the largest trunk available to carry all the gear. We soon learned that the young women who manned the rental car booths there tended to be attractive and friendly. They also seemed to like us news guys from out of town. In those days of racial strife, most white people in Mississippi were less than pleased to have us there covering the black activists, so anybody who didn't curse or spit at us seemed like the Welcome Wagon.

Two camera-crew members from a northern ABC bureau somehow began to spend some off-duty time with the same rental car girl — Maxine or Martha or Melanie or something M-ish.

Apparently, several months passed without the two men realizing they were seeing the same girl. I knew it, and everybody in the rental car business in Jackson knew it. For all I knew, the FBI and the Klan knew it. But nobody squealed to either of the guys. I guess everybody just thought that long days and evenings of running from Klansmen put a body in the mood for some recreation and it wasn't anybody else's business.

One day after a long stint in Jackson, I realized that the two crew members were not speaking to each other. I went to the third crew member and asked what was going on.

"Well, you know they both are seeing Maxine [or whatever], right?" he asked.

"Yeah, so what?"

"Well, they found out about each other and they're mad as hell," he said.

I didn't have sense enough to let it drop there, so I pressed on, hoping to get my staff back to normal: "So what's the problem now?"

He burst out laughing, then managed to answer: "They both got the clap. From her."

So I was working with two guys who got a venereal disease from the same girl, but the kicker was they weren't fighting about that. Both of them were still mad, my third crew member explained, because the other guy was still seeing her!

■　■　■

It was the late sixties, and my assignment for ABC News was to cover a story for the Sunday night newscast on a public official in Texas who was accused of corruption. My three-man camera crew and I arrived in Del Rio on that dusty Sunday morning and met with the news director of a local TV station, the ABC affiliate at the time.

He knew the story inside-out, including all the players, so I asked his advice on how best to cover the arrival at the courthouse that day of the allegedly corrupt official.

"Hell, he could go in the front or the back. Who knows?" said the otherwise astute news director.

"I've only got one camera crew, so can you help us?" I asked, knowing that the local station would want coverage for its own newscast anyway.

"No problem," said the news director. "How about you network guys cover the front of the courthouse and I'll handle the back door, so either way, we won't miss him."

I was relieved. I didn't want to have to call the producer at ABC News in New York and tell him that my feed to the network that night about a headline-making corruption trial would not include footage of the main character in the drama.

So we waited. My network cameraman, soundman and lightman were ready, poised, fingers on the buttons and switches. I was calm, knowing the local guy was equally ready at the rear of the courthouse.

It was hot and muggy, a couple of minutes before 1:00 p.m. No bad guy. Then it was one o'clock straight up. Still no bad guy. At five minutes after, I said to the shooter, "Well, he must have gone in the back door. Stay here and get him if he shows; I'll go around and check it out."

As I rounded the second corner and walked toward the rear entrance of the courthouse, the Del Rio news director came walking toward me, a big grin on his face.

"No sweat, man. I got him clean, a great shot!"

"Great. Guess he thought he'd dodge us out front," I smiled. "Sure glad you guys were back here."

Then I realized that there were no "you guys" — just him.

"You did get him on film, right?"

"Sure did, clear as a bell," he beamed, and then he showed me. There was the corrupt official, all right, clear as a bell and looking appropriately grumpy, as he stared out at me from that Polaroid snapshot.

HAWKS

FLY

By rights the Atlanta Hawks should be the Louisville Hawks by now. They would be, were it not for two men. One is Ted Turner. The other is Hubie Brown. When Ted bought the Hawks to save them from departing, he brought in Hubie from the old American Basketball Association, where he had coached the Louisville team in that league to a championship.

The Hawks had very little money, which worked out okay because they didn't have many good players to pay the money to. They went so far as to sign a little 5'-6" guard named Charlie Criss out of the Eastern League. Charlie was twenty-eight years old and had been working as a delivery person before he got his chance with the Hawks. Also on the roster were young, green kids like John Drew, Eddie Johnson and Wayne "Tree" Rollins. The Hawks' only star at the time was Lou Hudson.

The Hawks had the lowest payroll in the league and were predicted by everyone to finish in last place. Hubie Brown took those kids and turned them into a .500 team that made the playoffs. It was the most fun I ever had broadcasting basketball, watching those kids over-achieve all year. Hubie was the kind of coach who whipped them on, and his team responded to him. So did the fans. There was virtually no one in attendance at the start of the year, but as the season progressed, the whole city got fired up.

We called them the cardiac kids. In virtually every game they were up against teams that, on paper, should have beaten them by twenty points. Hubie's assistant coach was Frank Layden, a good basketball man, a delightful person, and a man who has done well with a part-time acting career between coaching gigs. Layden, with his sense of humor, was a counterpoint to Hubie, who could be, as they say, abrasive.

A guy who frustrated Brown beyond all reason was John Drew, a kid with unlimited talent but who enjoyed every moment of the fame and recognition his basketball abilities brought him. John stayed up even later than I did.

One night we're playing the Knicks in Madison Square Garden. It's a close one. In the third quarter the Hawks lead by one. Bill Bradley runs a backdoor play on Drew and makes a layup. New York by one. We score at the other end. Atlanta by one. Bradley backdoors Drew again. New York by one. Drew hits a 25-footer. Atlanta by one. Bradley backdoors Drew yet again for another layup. New York by one. As Drew jogs back down the floor, Hubie drops into his characteristic courtside pose, down on one knee, and from between cupped hands he screams, "Will you get into the bleeping game?"

Unfortunately for the Hawks, John sometimes forgot to hustle. He was moving so slowly that he was passed by referee Kenny Faulkner. Faulkner, naturally, being the closest to Hubie, thought the outburst was directed at him. Technical Brown — his second of the night — and he's ejected. He went ballistic, naturally, until he turned to me broadcasting from right next to him on the Garden floor. I was laughing so hard I was crying. Then Drew, trying to explain, grabs Faulkner and says, "Kenny, he was talking to ME. That's the way he ALWAYS talks to me." Even Hubie had to laugh as he departed for the dressing room.

WATCHING CHARLIE CRISS THAT YEAR was so much fun. Here was a guy who had been out of college for seven years. He was playing two games a week for $50 per game and trying to support a family delivering packages in Manhattan. Suddenly he is flying first class on commercial jets, making great money, getting good meals, and becoming one of Atlanta's most popular sports figures. Unlike so many sullen jocks you see and read about, here was a guy who enjoyed each and every minute of his professional life. Each day was like another Christmas for Charlie Criss that year, and his infectious laugh will never be forgotten by any of us who were involved with that team.

As you might expect, the Hawks' success brought those kids more fame and more money. In the next couple of years they began tiring of Hubie's tirades and simply tuned him out during time-outs and at halftime. As they tuned him out, Hubie became more abrasive, and he was gone after three years.

■ ■ ■

One of my favorite Hawks players of all time was Jumpin' Joe Caldwell out of the mean streets of Los Angeles and Arizona State University. Joe was a real gamer. He was a defensive specialist in the years when, like now, the big money normally went to the offensive stars.

I'll never forget a night when Joe and the Hawks were playing the Lakers in Atlanta in the days when Los Angeles featured Jerry West. West was Caldwell's assignment, and all you ever asked a guy when he was guarding West was to make him work for everything he got. You didn't expect to stop him, but you tried to keep him from taking over the entire game. Joe was so obsessed with his assignment that he even followed West to the Laker bench when a timeout was called. He wasn't show-boating . . . he was just so focused on West that he didn't realize that timeout had been called.

Skip with the Hawks' Joe Caldwell during the 1970 season.
(Courtesy Atlanta Journal-Constitution*)*

I think the Hawks might have become world champions and might have built a true dynasty if the team had been able to afford to keep Caldwell when they signed "Pistol Pete" Maravich. Maravich and Caldwell were good friends; they had done some camps together and that would have helped. Both loved to run. That would have helped. Both wanted to win. That would have helped. And neither one of them gave two hoots about race. That would have really helped.

■ ■ ■

Pistol Pete obviously came to Atlanta as the great white hope. It was a smart business move for a team trying to make it in the Deep South, but the whole situation was almost impossible for the Pistol. He was the so-called white superstar on a talented and predominantly black team — and he was called a superstar before he ever played a minute in the NBA. His teammates resented the Pistol. They would have been more than human had they not. He was doomed before he got started. And let's be honest — at LSU Pete was the whole show. He was the offense. Every night was showtime, and while victories were nice, the show was perhaps even more important. It doesn't work like that in the NBA.

Pete had a tough time adjusting to the fact that Lou Hudson could shoot the ball, too. And defense was something Pete had never been asked to play at LSU. Learning to play it against NBA stars was a tough row to hoe. Maravich was a kid who wanted to win but had never really been taught how to blend his game with the talents of his teammates. Still, he was a helluva player and every night he would do something to amaze you. At Chicago Stadium I saw him score twenty-one fourth-quarter points against the guard tandem of Jerry Sloan and Norm Van Lier — without much doubt the best guard tandem in the league defensively.

Pete was never a really happy kid with the Hawks, but later in life he became a born-again Christian and was a truly happy and contented man. That's what made his untimely death so doubly tragic. He had chased all the demons away and was having more fun playing the game for nothing than he had ever had playing it for money. All who knew him well miss him still. He was a quality person.

■ ■ ■

Two of the Hawks I really liked and admired in the early days were Lenny Wilkens and Paul Silas. Lenny was the captain of the team when I was first named as the broadcaster back in 1966 in St. Louis. I was replacing a broadcaster named Jerry Gross who had been a close friend of Lenny's and whose departure was not of his own volition. It would have been easy for Wilkens to make it tough on the new guy because of his friendship with the old one, but he never did. He told me, in fact, that while he liked Gross, he knew I didn't have anything to do with his departure, and anything he could do to help me he would do. With his friendship and that of Coach Richie Guerin, my rookie year was like a dream come true. Of course, winning sixteen of the first seventeen games didn't hurt.

Former team captain and current Hawks coach Lenny Wilkens.
(Courtesy Turner Broadcastem System)

Silas was one of those guys who you meet and instantly know is your friend. We've been friends ever since. He was a terrible shooter, but a brilliant rebounder and defender. Silas knew how to play the game and was a class individual. When the Hawks traded him (for a guy who couldn't hold his jockstrap), it was the only time I felt like crying. The trade was a total disaster and severely hurt the team's chances. Silas is black, and the kid we got for him, Gary Gregor, is white. Nobody admitted that race had anything to do with the deal, but there was really no other reason for such a trade to have been made.

■ ■ ■

Speaking of race, traveling with a pro basketball team in the '60s and '70s was a great education in that regard. The black guys were the primary heroes, and in our little world they were in the majority. In those days we would sit and argue about civil rights and civil disturbances by the hour. My writer friend, Frank Hyland, and I would go nose-to-nose with guys like Silas, Bill Bridges, Walt Hazzard, and Zelmo Beaty. It was a tremendous learning experience for both whites and blacks, and I'm sorry to say I don't see as much of it anymore around sports. It always seemed to me that frank exchanges of ideas could do nothing but help.

When the Hawks first moved to Atlanta they had a black starting lineup with Caldwell, Bridges, Beaty, Hazzard, and Lou Hudson. I never even thought about it, but from the tone of my early mail in Atlanta, a lot of other folks did. I was called a "nigger lover" and worse many times. I used to show the mail to the players, and we would laugh about it. Not because it was funny, but what else could you do? There were a few death threats thrown in — but nothing more serious than the threats ever occurred. It's interesting to learn that once you get to know a person as a person, his or her race is something you really don't think about. There's a lesson in there for all of us of all races, I think.

CAIRO

CHRISTMAS

When my boss told me about this assignment, I assumed it was a consolation prize. I was to go to Cairo, Egypt, and stay there about a month, over Christmas, to cover whatever happened.

Absolutely nothing was going on there at the time, and our regular Cairo correspondent wanted some time off from the boredom. Still, I had never been to Egypt, so I pretended to myself that it really was my idea, not that of the ABC News brass in New York.

December of 1970 turned out to be one of the rainiest months in the history of Egypt, and, as you know, Egypt goes way back. The rain meant that Cairo's already paralytic traffic was even worse than normal. All the water had dislodged a lot of the motor oil residue and other crud on the streets, making them slick as glass. If I had been there as a traffic reporter, I'd have been a smash hit.

Canada Dry and his handlers arrive for "Christmas in Cairo," 1971.

So I spent most of my thirty-seven days there riding in an ABC News hired taxi an hour or so each way to and from the Ministry of Information. It was only about two miles from the hotel but it took forever.

The rest of each day was spent inside the Ministry of Information, waiting to get some information. Usually all I got was a "no comment." After all, this was Sadat's Egypt of 1970, still Israel's arch enemy, still a tightly run state where freedom of the press was as alien as an icicle.

My daily request for permission to travel around the country and do stories was denied. One of the Ministry of Information guys actually told me that filming sand was prohibited. Sand? About ninety percent of Egypt is sand, so that restriction gave me more time to spend in traffic.

One day I forsook the round-trip to information hell to poke around along the banks of the Nile River. I enjoyed watching the graceful *felucca* go by, the boats that give the Nile some of its charm. I wandered over to a fruit stand about a block from the river. Plump, juicy grapefruits and oranges were on display. Mmmm, mmmm good.

Then I noticed a guy behind the fruit stand with a bucket of water and a pile of citrus fruit. He also had a syringe in his hand. I looked closer. Sure enough, he was injecting water into the fruit to plump it up. The water, needless to say, came from the Nile — the famous, historic, and really polluted Nile. We decided against the fruit cocktail at dinner that night in the hotel restaurant.

My calendar told me that Christmas was coming, but the rain pelting the mosques and minarets of Cairo gave off no such message. December 25 would be just another day in this Moslem country. That sad fact, combined with my lack-of-news-induced torpor, made the prospects for the holiday pretty dismal.

Suddenly that outlook changed with the kindness of a Canadian reporter friend, Don North. Don, his wife, and three children lived in Cairo in a neighborhood popular with diplomats and other foreigners. They had a big family, a big house, and big plans for Christmas Day. They invited several of us foreign strays to join them for a holiday dinner, North American style.

My delight was countered by a dilemma: What kind of Christmas present can you buy Canadian kids, ages eight to eleven, when your shopping is limited to the souk, the Arab market? The ever-popular hookah? Nope, wrong age group. I next considered getting them a camel saddle, but for kids who probably missed having pony rides, that seemed a bit off the mark.

Then it dawned on me. Earlier that month I had visited the pyramids at Giza, just outside Cairo, and had noticed a guy with a camel selling rides on the beast to tourists. I returned the day before Christmas and found that I could rent Canada Dry (that was the camel's name) for Christmas Day. I've forgotten the cost, but it wasn't bad, no doubt less than importing a pony for the day.

THE NEXT MORNING, CHRISTMAS DAY, I arrived at the North's house with no gifts in hand. The kids were polite and well-behaved and pretended not to notice. Then I heard some neighbor children outside making a lot of noise. We all trooped outside, where the object of the clamor was apparent. I had given good directions; the camel had arrived.

The camel rides were a big hit and, by association, so was I. Even the children's mother relaxed after the first child made it on and off Canada Dry safely.

The kids didn't need Rudolph, nor Dancer or Prancer or Comet or the rest. They had a hissing, ornery, one-humped camel and a ticket to ride, from me.

Our Christmas party never made "The ABC Evening News" that night. We didn't even film it. But I daresay it was one of the nicer events in that part of the world on that Christmas Day.

ON *the* ROAD...
AGAIN

HO, HO,

HO CHI

MINH

Saturday, February 13, 1971, was one of the luckiest and unluckiest days of my life, but I didn't know about the lucky part until it was over. On that hot, dangerous day in Southeast Asia, I escaped death by the flip of a coin and landed by accident on the Ho Chi Minh Trail.

In Vietnam for ABC News, I was one of many correspondents chasing the story of the U.S.-backed South Vietnamese excursion into Laos. Officially, it wasn't happening, of course. A lot of people got killed in incidents that "never happened" in that war.

But the operation had a name, Lam Song 719, and a purpose, to interdict North Vietnamese troops moving along the Ho Chi Minh Trail. About 6:00 a.m. on that Saturday, other reporters and TV crews and I gathered on the tarmac at the airstrip at Quang Tri in the northern part of South Vietnam. We did that almost every day, trying to hitch helicopter rides into Laos, to cover the action.

Most days, we all made it onto choppers, the Huey transport gunships that were the workhorses of that war. That Saturday morning, however, too many media folks were wanting rides on too few helicopters, so we flipped coins to see who went first.

I lost, so my crew and I had to watch as the first press chopper took off, carrying ace photographer Larry Burroughs and three other veteran journalists. I lost a second coin toss, and another chopper took off with reporters aboard, heading for Laos. We finally made it on the third chopper, along with CBS News correspondent Don Webster and his two-man film crew.

Did I mention that these helicopters were operated by South Vietnamese pilots?

Choppers are scary enough, but choppers flown by South Vietnamese crews were especially frightening. They just didn't have the skill or experience of their U.S. flyboy counterparts.

We went anyway. It was the only way to get to the action inside Laos.

I knew we were in trouble even before we left the ground. As we strapped ourselves into the chopper, the pilot jumped out of the

Don and cameraman Terry Khoo in Vietnam in 1971. Khoo was killed shortly before his tour of duty for ABC News was to end.

cockpit, walked to the front of the Huey and wrote some map coordinates on the glass with grease pencil. Get the picture: standing out there, looking back into the chopper, he wrote the map coordinates so he could read them, out there. Of course, when he got back into the pilot's seat, the coordinates were written backwards.

He shrugged it off and we took off.

We were lost in no time. The pilot was radioing for assistance from the two choppers that had left before us, hoping they had found the landing zone. No radio contact. Nothing.

As we got low on fuel, the Vietnamese pilot began looking for a safe place to land in what clearly was enemy territory. Suddenly he veered to the right, put the nose toward the ground and swooped into a clearing. With the chopper still several feet off the ground, he motioned us out. We jumped to the ground and looked back, wondering where he was going. He gestured and shouted something about getting fuel and returning, then swept up and away before he could draw enemy fire.

We ran out of the clearing into the nearby woods and listened, sweating now, knowing we were in Laos, with no good guys anywhere near us. Nothing. Quiet. After five or ten minutes, we moved out along a small path, heading west. Suddenly that path merged with a much larger path, an obviously well-worn north-south trail with a lot of small tributaries.

Above our heads, the taller trees had been pulled to the center and tied together, to form a canopy of branches and leaves. The trail was not visible from the air. In the dirt, we saw tracks from narrow tires, mortars or small artillery pieces perhaps, and a lot of footprints.

And about every 100 yards or so we saw holes in the ground on the right side of the trail. The holes were about thirty inches in diameter and about five feet deep.

Webster and I were puzzled about what we saw and where we were, but his Vietnamese cameraman cleared it up for us real fast.

"Ho Chi Minh Trail," he said, without expression.

"You gotta be kidding," I said, and Webster grinned the grin of the deeply afraid. I was too scared to grin.

And that's what it was — one of the many small pathways and trails cut through the jungle that made up what we in the West called by the monolithic name, Ho Chi Minh Trail.

As far as we knew, we were the first American journalists ever to take a walk along that famous route of America's enemy. Its multiple paths wandered through Vietnam and nearby Laos, mile after mile. The jungle canopy was to keep American warplanes from seeing the troop movements. Those deep holes along the path were for North Vietnamese soldiers to jump into for protection when bombs began to fall.

We filmed everything, Webster and I both wishing that the other network guy was not along on this trip.

At one point, Don saw a crude painted sign nailed to a tree on the side of the path. He ran over and yanked it off. My Korean cameraman and Vietnamese soundman hit the ground, covering their heads.

When I asked what the hell they were doing, they stood and shook their heads.

"Booby trap, could be booby trap," my soundman said.

If it had been, Webster would have been the story that day.

A mile or so further on, I saw another sign, nailed to a tree at a crossroads in the trail. "Duong Ra," it read, with an arrow painted red on a raw piece of lumber.

This sign was mine, no booby trap this time either. I put it in my pack, brought it home, and still have it today.

We retraced our steps and made it back to the clearing, hoping our South Vietnamese chopper pilot really would come back for us. After we waited about two hours in the hot sun, he did, sweeping in, hollering for us to hurry, and zooming out of there while we were still scrambling aboard.

I was exhilarated. I had a film story of the Ho Chi Minh trail and apparently was going to live to get it on the air.

Back in Quang Tri, Webster and I raced to a field phone to call our Saigon bureaus and tell them what we had. We wrote scripts and arranged for the film to be flown back to Saigon.

It was a couple of hours later, in the mess hall at dinner, that I learned what had happened to the other two press helicopters that day. Then I knew why we were not able to make radio contact when we had tried earlier. They were over Laos, in enemy territory, and got lost. The two choppers collided and crashed. All aboard died.

They had won the coin toss that my crew and I had lost.

■　■　■

When Peter Jennings offered to let me stay at his place in Rome on my way home from Vietnam, I wasn't sure quite what to expect. He said the *super attico* would be free and I was welcome to use it. I envisioned myself all alone in a little attic room in a small flat, not your idyllic idea of a few days in the Eternal City.

Peter was the Rome correspondent for ABC News at that time, 1971, but he was in the Middle East for weeks and sometimes months at a stretch.

"Look, the place is available, and you won't be any trouble," he told me. "In fact, I won't even be in town that week, so why not stay there?"

Peter's good friend and mine, ABC News correspondent Barrie Dunsmore, had shared the place with Peter for a time, and he too urged me to stay there. I left Saigon on Thursday, April 22, and after a day and night in Hong Kong, I flew via Rangoon, Burma (now Myanmar), to Rome.

The cab driver took me to the ABC News Bureau. I had learned how to say the address in Italian — *Venti cinque Via Abruzzi* — 25 Abruzzi Way. It was the only phrase I knew in Italian at that time; good thing the bureau had not changed addresses while I was in Vietnam. The key to the apartment was waiting for me there, with a note from Barrie inviting me to use it as long as I wished.

"Piazza Santa Maria in Trastevere," I said to the cabbie, who declined to proceed until he saw the address written on my note from Barrie and Peter. Then he drove there like an Indy purse was at stake.

Piazza Santa Maria is a quaint, lovely square in the Trastevere section of Rome, across the Tiber River. (Trastevere means literally, "across the Tiber.") An old lady sat at an outdoor cafe near the street entrance to the upstairs apartment. She was watching the ornate fountain in the middle of the square, but she turned to stare at me briefly as I got out of the cab. I nodded at her and smiled. She shrugged and turned her gaze back to the fountain. I glanced up and down the building, then went in.

"Hello, hello, anybody home?" I called as I opened the door. Barrie had told me that somebody might be there; he wasn't sure.

No one answered.

The main level, the *attico*, had a bedroom off the living room and an airy kitchen. But Barrie had told me to use the *super attico*, the room he used when he was in residence.

I dropped my bags and looked around. There was the bedroom, the living room, the kitchen, a bathroom, and a stairway up to a second level, containing a small hallway with bookshelves on the wall. I couldn't find a second bedroom, but I found the phone and called the ABC News bureau.

"This is embarrassing, but I can't find the *super attico* in Peter's apartment," I said to the Italian woman who answered the phones there.

"Oh yes," she said, "the *super attico*." She laughed as she explained that I had to press a panel in the bookcase to find the *super attico*. I got it on the second try. The bookcase swung around with but a slight push, just like in those Nick and Nora Charles drawing-room mystery movies, revealing a bedroom. I had found the *super attico*.

It was nice, a queen-sized bed, a bathroom adjoining. It would be a great place to stay, but I propped a flight bag against the bookcase to make sure it wouldn't slam shut and trap me in the *super attico* forever.

A few minutes later, the parade of Peter's friends began. "Allo, allo," a woman's voice called out, while I was in the bathroom.

"Hello," I yelled back, drying my hands and walking toward the revolving bookcase.

She was tall, dark-haired, lovely and laughing. "I see you found the secret door," she chuckled. "I am a friend of Peter's, and I'm staying here for a few days."

We shook hands and she explained that since I had taken the *super attico*, she would use the downstairs bedroom. Her name was Martishia, and she seemed absolutely unsurprised that I was there.

"Oh, Peter allows all his friends to use the apartment when he's not here," she told me.

I didn't see much of Martishia during the four days I stayed there, but I met a lot of Peter's other friends. The lady was right — Peter Jennings is a generous man who extended the use of his place to many, many people. Some of them had been there before and knew to expect a crowd. Others, including me, had assumed they were among a select few who had the key to "the place in Trastevere."

I didn't feel quite as special, once the flood of Peter's friends began to swell, but I had a great time and have fond memories of those days in Rome.

Barrie Dunsmore also has special memories of the *super attico*. One night while he was there, he went to sleep alone and awoke with an attractive woman in his bed. She had surprised Peter when she arrived very late the night before, using her own key to get in. Since he was already with a "friend" in the main bedroom, Peter — ever the hospitable host — suggested that she use the *super attico*. He failed to remember that Barrie was there, sound asleep.

Barrie had no idea who she was, so he dressed quietly that morning, not wanting to wake her and have to introduce himself.

It was that sort of place — all above-board, all friendly, urbane, interesting people — all with keys to Peter's apartment. Every night when I returned after an evening on the town, I would find different people there, or more than were there the night before. Not all stayed over, of course, but they came and went, meeting, greeting, leaving with a wave and a *ciao*.

The key to the chemistry of the place was Peter. Everybody liked him very much, and even when he was not there, which was most of the time, that place in Piazza Santa Maria had the feeling of a reunion of strangers-become-friends.

As I left four days later to catch a plane to Paris, that same old lady was sitting in the piazza, looking at the fountain, drinking coffee, eating a pastry. She saw me, shrugged again, and looked at the pigeons that had gathered for crumbs. A stranger at Peter's place was about as unusual as the pigeons in the square. Who knows, he may have invited the birds, too.

PLANES,

BUSES, &

PATROL

CARS

Broadcasting pro sports means you get to log a lot of time on airplanes, so naturally you get to witness some rather strange goings-on. I recall one baseball charter on which a player who shall remain nameless thought it would be a good idea to borrow a stewardess's lipstick and write on the lavatory mirror that there was a bomb on board the plane. Some law-abiding flight attendant reported the idiot, and an FBI investigation soon followed. The player soon departed for greener pastures.

Sometimes, though, the problem can start with the flight crew. I recall a commercial flight the Hawks were on during my tenure there. We had lost a tough game to the 76ers the night before and were on something like a 7:30 a.m. flight back to Atlanta for a game that night. Naturally, nobody had gotten much sleep. One of our players, Jeff Halliburton, went to his seat, fastened his seatbelt, pulled a blanket over his head and went to sleep.

The world's youngest flight attendant came by a few minutes later and tried to wake him to ask him if he wanted any coffee. From across the aisle I suggested that she let the kid sleep. She informed me in no uncertain terms that she had a job to do. Providing coffee for sleeping people was apparently her holy grail. She finally woke him and asked if he wanted coffee. His reply made sense. Why would a person trying to sleep want coffee to wake him up? He went back to sleep.

The same lady materialized five minutes later — just as we were getting ready to pull back from the gate — to ask him what his destination was. In frustration he snapped, "Havana." Bingo. Back to the gate we went. Jeff was pulled off the plane, and after about a two-hour delay, we departed without him. He made it by game time. The stewardess who caused the thing in the first place has since, in all likelihood, become an ardent feminist.

■   ■   ■

There is one airline story that I have been trying to live down for fifteen years because it isn't true — at least, if it is I wasn't involved. A disc jockey in Atlanta pinned it on me, however, and I still meet people who swear it's true.

Seems a commercial airliner has taken off from Atlanta's Hartsfield International Airport. As is always the case, the captain comes on with his usual P.A. announcement — words to the effect of, "Good evening folks, this is Captain Swanson. Welcome to Widget Airlines flight 789 non-stop startstream service to Philadelphia. We are climbing through 12,000 feet on our way to a cruising altitude of 33,000. The weather en route looks good and we expect an on-time arrival in Philadelphia at 8:45. So sit back, relax, and enjoy your flight."

The captain, so the story goes, then forgets to turn off his microphone and is heard by one and all saying, "Okay, now all I need is a cup of coffee and some oral sex." A stewardess, in blind panic, comes rushing from the back of the plane to tell the captain he's still on the air. The story goes that as she rushes by me I blurt out, "Hey, don't forget the coffee!"

I swear to God it never happened. I was never on any such flight. Never heard anything like that. But I've got to tell you, if I had heard it, I hope I would have been that quick. But I say again . . . it just isn't true.

■ ■ ■

Atlanta has a good bit of fog during the winter months, and most of it seems to hang around our airport. We were flying back to Atlanta with the Hawks one day when the airport was closed, so we diverted to Chattanooga. The weather kept deteriorating so it was decided that we would bus the rest of the way to Atlanta to play our game against the Buffalo Braves that night. They were in town waiting for us.

Away we went. All was well until the bus caught fire halfway between Chattanooga and Atlanta, stranding us by the roadside. Bud Seretean, then our chairman of the board, came driving by and promised he would find help for us, but before his help arrived, a bus full of evangelists pulled up and offered assistance. They were a traveling musical show.

I clambered on the bus and went for help. Why me? I was the only one not afraid to do it. We finally found a highway patrolman who radioed some of his mates. By now it was close to game time.

Off went the Atlanta Hawks in four Georgia State Patrol cars at speeds well over 100 mph. We convinced them that the game wasn't that important after all, that it was *really* OK with us if they slowed down a little. We got to the court an hour late, but still managed to kick Buffalo's butt.

■　■　■

A chartered bus hurtles down the highway in the dead of night. It is the Atlanta Braves, after a night game, heading for their next port of call. Suddenly, the distinctive sound of a police siren is heard, just barely, over the normal conversation. In a panic the bus driver slows and checks his mirror. By now, no siren and no sight of a police car. He speeds up again and once again hears the siren, a little louder this time. Again he slows and checks his mirror, but sees nothing.

It happens every time you get a new bussie. Steve Bedrosian has struck again. The man can pitch. He can also sound exactly like a police car, a power saw, and any number of other things that a "normal" person could never learn how to do. Bedrock has been a relief pitcher for a long time.

■　■　■

There are always some great stories to tell by the end of a season about trying to move a party of fifty or thereabouts around the country. Our traveling secretary, Bill Acree, does a marvelous job — and all of us deeply appreciate how easy he makes things for us, but like all else in life, things don't always go the way you plan.

I remember a terrible day in 1983 in Los Angeles. We blew a three-run ninth-inning lead when Claudell Washington lost a ball in the sun. That loss on a Sunday afternoon just about put the lid on the Braves' attempt to win consecutive divisional titles in '82 and '83. We boarded our charter flight to Cincinnati not in the best of moods.

As we entered the plane, the fuel nozzle that was gassing us up went berserk. Gasoline was flying everywhere, and we were ordered to deplane immediately. We waited around about an hour while they soaked up the gasoline off the runway, then boarded again and the same thing happened. It seems that a fuel gauge was malfunctioning; the tanks were full when the gauge showed them half empty. Another hour-and-a-half wait ensued. Because of the fuel problem, they were afraid to gas the tanks completely, so we got to stop for fuel in Kansas City. A three-hour flight had turned into about nine hours, and we didn't touch down in Cincinnati until nine in the morning. Thank God it was an off day.

■ ■ ■

Another horror story occurred when we outsmarted ourselves — and I think it was my fault. Another Sunday game in Los Angeles, late in (I think) the 1984 season, and we were headed home after the game. On that day the Rams were playing at home, the Raiders were playing at home, there was a big auto race, and the Dodgers had another of their sellout crowds. To say that traffic was rough in LA was an understatement.

I suggested to Acree, "You know, it's a shame we can't leave from a different airport to avoid all the turmoil and traffic." Poor Billy. He thought I was on to something, so he arranged for us to leave from the Burbank Airport, which would save us about an hour in commute time. That was the plan.

Our friends at Delta had just purchased Western Airlines and were integrating some of the Western personnel into the Delta family. Could a 727 with fifty people take off from the Burbank Airport on a charter? Sure, said the former Western folks. They were right. Fifty people was no problem. What was a problem, however, was that these fifty people had been on a two-week roadtrip and had a lot of luggage. Also, twenty-five of these people were baseball players, all of whom had canvas bags full of bats and balls and gloves and catching equipment. There were also two trainers with about a ton of medical supplies.

To heighten the mood of the day we had lost again, and the caterers had neglected to load any beer, any ice, or any soft drinks on board. When they weighed us in, they discovered that we could take off alright, but not if we wanted to live. Too much weight. They had to offload all the equipment and ship it back to LAX. We were delayed about three hours. Had Acree had his way, I would have been allowed to deplane somewhere over the Rockies at about 33,000 feet. But it had seemed like such a swell idea.

■ ■ ■

Without question, the funniest trip I've ever been on was on a bus back in the '70s when the Braves were horrible. We were flying into Philadelphia on the day of the game to take on the Phillies. It was the middle of the summer; the temperature when we arrived was about 95 degrees, and the bus that showed up to meet us had no air-conditioning. A new bridge had just opened in Philadelphia, and our driver was going that way until he spotted a sign that said no trucks or buses. He panicked and pulled off onto the only access road he could find. Unfortunately for him (and for us), the road apparently led to nowhere. We were driving around in a kind of swamp between the airport and this huge mountain of demolished cars. To make matters worse, our driver was a fellow of Spanish extraction who spoke almost no English. Our bus was one of those old city buses with the cord you could pull when you wanted to get off. After about fifteen minutes of trying fruitlessly to extricate himself from the swamp, our bussie pulled up to a big pool of standing water — nearly a lake. Just then Darrel Chaney hit the cord and announced, "Swamp and lake, everybody out."

Our manager in those days, Dave Bristol, was a man with a short fuse in any situation, and in this one — what with the heat, the sweat, and a lousy ballclub — he went ballistic. "How does it feel," asked Dave, "to drive around down here making an ass out of yourself." By now the bus is in hysterics, the driver is about to try to kill Bristol, and we are lost by this fetid lake. Fortunately, Mike Marshall was on the trip. The first thing he did was to quiet down Willie Montanez — our only Latin player — who was making everything worse by berating this poor guy in español. Then Marshall, using his high school Spanish, helped the guy to find his way back to civilization. I'll never forget sitting there trying not to laugh while Bristol, dressed in a dark suit no less, fumed away. It was funny to everyone but Dave.

■　■　■

Then there was our limousine ride from Philadelphia to New York. Sutton, Simpson, Van Wieren, our radio producer/engineer Rick Shaw, and I had convinced TBS to rent us a limo after a day game in Philadelphia to take us to New York. Our talent coordinator in those days — the lovely and accomplished Michele

Zarzaca — outdid herself. Not only was there a limo, but there was a limo filled with libations, so that each of us could enjoy his beverage of choice for the nearly three-hour trip.

The first two hours went quickly enough, but then Van Wieren announced a need to relieve himself. Our driver was stuck in horrible traffic, and we were thirty miles from the next rest stop. Once Pete mentioned it, all of us became very interested in venting our bladders. Finally, in desperation, we found a small construction workers' building and were lined up there beside the brutal traffic, *praying* that the team bus didn't ride by and catch us in the act.

Skip's boon companion (and fellow Braves announcer) Pete Van Wieren.
(Courtesy Turner Broadcasting System)

When we reached the Holland Tunnel, the traffic was a disaster and so were we. Van Wieren was busily smoking his 467th cigarette of the trip, and Simpson, for the 467th time, rolled down a window so we wouldn't all die. "Hi, guys," said Braves pitcher Kent Mercker. He and his wife, Julie, were in the limousine next to ours. Very cleverly I ad-libbed, "Pardon me, but do you have any Grey Poupon?" Without a word, Mercker handed us a bottle of the stuff, causing roughly 2,000,000 commuters to stop their cars and start looking for the television cameras.

■　■　■

Some trips that start out deadly serious turn out to be laugh riots before they're over with. Several years ago I was diagnosed with arrhythmia — in layman's terms, an irregular heartbeat. It's under control now with medication, but that day in Los Angeles is one I will never forget.

I was sitting in my room reading the *L.A. Times* when suddenly

I noticed that my heart was beating at about twice its normal rate. I quickly headed to the ballpark where our trainers, Dave Pursley and Jeff Porter, were already at work on some of the players' lingering injuries. One listen to my ticker and they made immediate plans to get me to a hospital. It is now about five o'clock on a weekday afternoon in Los Angeles. A dear friend of mine — our then stage manager Richard Croker — happened into the clubhouse about that time and volunteered to drive me. We got directions from the Dodger medical staff and off we went.

In ten minutes we were lost in the Mexican barrio which adjoins downtown. We couldn't find anyone who spoke English, and neither of us spoke any Spanish. In desperation, after about twenty cries of "DONDE ESTA EL HOSPITAL!" brought no meaningful response, Croker in frustration began asking in German, a language he picked up while serving over there in the military. Somehow the whole thing started to strike me funny. I started laughing and couldn't stop. I laughed so hard, in fact, that I somehow popped my heart back into the correct rhythm.

By now the normally unflappable Croker is a basket case. He's driving around with a 250-pound lunatic who is perhaps dying of a heart attack and having a wonderful time about it. Finally we find a hospital — I don't think it was the one we were looking for. Our doctor turns out to be a guy from Pakistan who speaks even less English than the fellows we were asking directions from. Croker and I both begin laughing and Richard starts talking to the Pakistani in German. It was wonderful. The doctor was so frazzled after five minutes with us that we thought he might need a bed in his own hospital.

■   ■   ■

I must admit, though, that after years of flying commercially with the Atlanta Hawks, coming to baseball spoiled me rotten. In the last decade or so almost all of the trips have become charters. Say we are leaving Atlanta on a Thursday off-day to play in New York on Friday. You drive to the ballpark, drive into the tunnel, and pull up to the clubhouse. One of the equipment guys grabs your bag, and you keep driving until you find a place to park. Then you wander back to the clubhouse and wait thirty minutes for a couple of buses to materialize in the tunnel. They whisk you to the airport and, in most cities, deliver you right to the plane sitting on the tarmac.

Soon you are airborne, and often wined and dined. You deplane in New York, walk five steps and get on a bus, and go straight to your hotel, where your key and a rooming list are both waiting for you. Off you go to your room (or wherever) and thirty minutes later — as if by magic — your luggage appears in your room. It's a lot different from the stress you can go through with commercial flights, and, as I said, it's easy to get spoiled.

WELCOME TO BELFAST

The notice was typed on a sheet of laminated paper, lying on the desk in the hotel room. I dropped my bag on the bed and picked up the notice to read it.

"Because of the difficulties, it may be necessary for our guests to evacuate the hotel on short . . ."

That's as far as I got.

Ka-BOOM!!!

A blast from somewhere nearby knocked me to the floor. It blew out the windows in the hotel room and the glass covered me and the floor. My head cleared, and I started to stand up just as someone began pounding on my hotel room door. I tiptoed across the shards of glass and opened the door.

There stood Jim Godfrey, my ABC News cameraman, his arm around a shaking, bloody chambermaid, a frightened girl no more than eighteen years old.

"Welcome to Northern Ireland," said Jim, a Briton who had been to Belfast many times before. "Can we come in, then?"

We were in the Europa Hotel in Belfast. It was about the nicest hotel in that city, and it was in the middle of insanity, a crazy quilt of blood and revenge, hatred and death, that had been going on for centuries.

Covering the recurring carnage in Northern Ireland is one of the bad things, probably the worst thing, about being a correspondent based in London for an American television network.

The year was 1972, early autumn. The leaves were long gone from the trees in downtown Belfast. Most of the trees were gone too, lost in the crossfire of a thousand bullets between violent Catholics and Protestants. They disagree on who should govern Northern Ireland and are willing to kill a lot of innocent people in the name of freedom or God or both.

This was my first of many trips to Northern Ireland, and I dreaded it. I had covered the war in Vietnam, the revolution in the Dominican Republic, and civil riots in Chicago, Philadelphia, and a half dozen other American cities, so I was no rookie to armed conflict. But Northern Ireland is different. You turn the ignition key in your rental car with a wince, wondering whether a car bomb will turn it and you into confetti.

The bartender draws you a cold one and you taste the beer gingerly, making sure that beer is all you can taste. Terrorist weapons of death come in many packages, many flavors. I had been in the country less than an hour, in my hotel room less than a minute, when that explosion blasted me into the reality of Northern Ireland.

"Jesus, what happened to her?" I asked Jim, as tears on the maid's face streaked into the trickles of blood coming from her hairline.

"We were standing by the window at the end of the hall when the bomb went off," Jim told me. The glass had sparkled her skin with tiny cuts.

They had been looking out to the parking lot between the hotel building and a train station nearby. A bomb had been planted in a car in the lot, and the terrorist had called the hotel with a warning. Hotel employees said the alarm system had not worked properly and they had not had time to call all of the rooms to alert guests to the bomb. Jim and I saw that the cuts on her face and arms were superficial. She was sobbing and scared, but all the blood made it look worse than it was.

I called the desk and asked for a doctor. Jim ran back to his room to get his camera and the soundman, Robin Springate, to go cover the car-bombing outside the hotel.

I brushed the broken glass off the desk and picked up that laminated notice I had been reading when the bomb went off. I read it again and was able to finish the message this time:

"Because of the difficulties, it may be necessary for our guests to evacuate the hotel on short notice. If you hear the warning bell, please leave your room immediately and walk down the stairs and out of the hotel. Please gather for further instructions in the car park next door."

It's a good thing nobody heard the faulty alarm system because the car park is where the bomb went off.

Welcome to Northern Ireland.

■ ■ ■

On another trip to Northern Ireland, I decided to do a feature story on some American social workers who were in Belfast trying to help the local children deal with the ravages of the war there.

We heard that the women were working in a second-floor apart-

Debris from the car-park explosion outside the Europa Hotel in Belfast, where Don was staying in 1972.

ment over a bar on the Falls Road. That was the center of the Roman Catholic stronghold in Belfast — a dangerous area for outsiders, especially Britons and journalists who lived in Britain. That included me, of course, and my British camera crew, Jim Godfrey and Robin Springate.

Jim and Robin were understandably skittish about the assignment.

"Um, do you know what bar that would be?" asked cameraman Godfrey, a frown on his usually smiling face.

"Yeah, they said it was the Long Bar," I replied, as we stood in the lobby of the Europa Hotel. "Funny name, Long Bar," I mused.

"Funny? You think that's funny?" piped up Robin Springate, the young, curly-haired, devil-may-care soundman. "Nothing funny about the Long Bar, mate!" said Robin.

Jim explained that the Long Bar was a notorious hangout for IRA terrorists, the toughest, most dangerous place on one of the toughest, most dangerous roads in the Catholic-controlled areas of Belfast. He suggested we might not want to wander down there just to do a feature on some American women on a mission.

I humored them into it, explaining that it was sure to make the evening news and that it would save us from having to go on a patrol with British soldiers that day, an exercise that would be as dangerous as anything could be in Belfast. So we phoned our driver, Paddy, and he picked us up in his new Volvo. Paddy was a Roman Catholic native of Northern Ireland. He knew the territory and he knew a lot of the people on both sides of the conflict.

In the Protestant areas, we were always careful to call him "Billy," rather than "Paddy," because "Paddy" was a popular Catholic name derived from Saint Patrick, the fifth-century apostle and patron saint of Ireland. "Billy," on the other hand, was a Protestant name, popular because of the sixteenth-century Protestant hero, William of Orange.

I figured Paddy was a good guy to have along on a trip to the Long Bar, and, what's more, he was willing to go. So we went, about noon on a Tuesday.

We pulled up in front of the place, and I told Jim and Robin to get their gear out while I went upstairs to check it out. I told them

I'd wait for them inside. I walked past the door to the Long Bar and into an open door leading to a stairway to the second floor.

The women and children were up there, in small groups, enjoying themselves with coloring books, song sheets, and various toys. I introduced myself, found the leader, explained why I was there, and added that my crew would be up in a moment.

Ten minutes went by, no Jim and Robin. Another ten minutes, no crew. I went down the stairs to find out what had kept them, and when I walked out of the doorway, I saw Jim, Robin, and Paddy standing by Paddy's new Volvo. A fourth man was there, a stranger. Nobody was talking.

"What's up, guys? We're late; let's go upstairs," I said.

Jim motioned me closer. "Well, we have a situation here," he said quietly, pointing to the stranger.

I looked at him. He reached into his belt, pulled out a long-barreled .45 revolver, and pointed it at my chest. He was only four feet away. I froze, then looked at Jim and managed to croak, "Um, what's the deal?"

"He wants Paddy's car, now," said Jim.

The guy with the gun then spoke, in an accent so thick I had trouble understanding him. He said he had a wounded comrade and had to get him to a safe house right away. He demanded our car.

Paddy then spoke up, his brogue thicker than I'd ever noticed before: "I just got this car, and it's my living, old son," he said to the IRA man.

"Sorry, but I've gotta have a car. My man's not doing well. Took two bullets."

Paddy was angry and the rest of us were scared silly. I offered the gunman an alternative.

"Look, don't take Paddy's car, OK? He needs it to feed his good Catholic family," I said. "But I've got a Hertz rental car back at the Europa Hotel, so how about Paddy takes us back there and I'll get the Ford and bring it here to you, OK?"

This guy was a terrorist, a gunman, but he wasn't stupid.

"Well, I'll take that car alright," he said to me, pointing the gun, "but you stay here with me. Send your driver and this man [Robin] to get the Ford."

Robin and Paddy agreed and moved to the car.

"And if you're not back in fifteen minutes, this bloke buys it," he said, waving the gun at me.

So there we were, my suave British cameraman, an armed IRA terrorist with a wounded pal waiting inside the Long Bar, and me, this young, dumb American reporter who wanted to do a feature story on American women and Irish kids having a nice time.

We stood there on the street, near the now empty curb, the gun back in the guy's waistband now, his eyes still on me. The ice age must have been shorter than the next eighteen minutes, which is how long it took Robin and Paddy to get back from the hotel with the rental car.

They could have called the police and stayed away, safe. That might have produced a shootout, however, with Jim and me as the shootees.

The IRA guy said, as he took the car keys, that we could fetch the car the next day at the corner of something and something. He then went into the Long Bar, and we went upstairs and did our feature story. When we came out, the Ford was gone and Paddy's Volvo was there, untouched. We sped back to the hotel, bursting with that indescribable rush you get when you flirt with death and live to laugh about it nervously with others who also survived.

We knew we'd never see that Hertz car again. Sure enough, it was exploded in a car-bombing the next day, after the IRA used it to transport the wounded man to get treatment.

I was nervous when I went to the Hertz counter at the Belfast airport at week's end to report the "loss" of the car.

"You're not going to believe this," I said to the perky Hertz lady at the check-in counter. "My car was hijacked at gunpoint, and I think they blew it up."

I figured that my employer, ABC News, or I would have to pay for it. The Hertz woman never even blinked.

"Oh, another one. OK, we have a form for that, so fill this out and keep one copy," she said as she pushed some paperwork across the counter at me.

"You have a form for people whose rental cars get hijacked at gunpoint?" I asked.

"Sure, happens all the time here. Is it your first, then?" she asked with a smile.

No wonder Hertz was Number One. They had a form for everything.

■　■　■

The bullets had been flying in Belfast that night. In the middle of the fray, trying to get a story to make some sense of the carnage in that pathetic place, were my two bosses at the time. They were the ABC News London bureau chief, George Watson, and the executive producer in the London bureau, Walter Porges.

They managed to avoid getting shot and made their way back through the police and British troops' roadblocks to the Europa Hotel, where most foreign journalists stayed while covering the ongoing war in Northern Ireland. They signed in and went to the bar, then to the dining room, hoping the kitchen was still open that nasty night. A sign at the entry to the restaurant made them laugh.

"Coat and Tie Required."

This hotel full of besieged, bedraggled journalists, in the middle of a war, was requiring coats and ties in order to eat dinner? In what at that hour, 11:00 p.m., was a virtually empty dining room? No way.

Way. Walter and George were stopped by an officious head waiter as they walked in, wearing the open-collared sport shirts and khakis in which they'd just trekked to the battlelines of the city.

"Sorry sir, you must not have seen our sign. You must wear a jacket and a tie," he said. Walter laughed again and George got a little snippy.

"You must be joking, sir!" George said, summoning some of his considerable dignity.

"No, it's the house rule, sorry."

"Young man," sniffed George, "we've just been in a bunker with the troops, just saw bullet holes in your sidewalk, just endured a thorough search by the troops at your front door. We are tired, we are hungry, and we are not terribly patient. Please enforce your rules about coats and ties tomorrow, but not tonight, because we WILL EAT HERE NOW!"

And they did. George had the lamb chops. Walter had the beef and a renewed respect for George's ability to wilt a waiter with a well-constructed paragraph.

ANOTHER SIGN I'LL ALWAYS remember from Belfast was the one on a four-foot pole, carried around the lobby and dining room of the Europa Hotel by a uniformed bellman. Whenever a guest got a phone call, the bellman would write the guest's name on the sign, ring his little bicycle handlebar bell, and shout the person's name.

"Mr. Smith, paging Mr. Smith," the bellman would call out, ringing the little bell, carrying the sign with pride, the way an Olympic athlete might carry the torch.

Mr. Smith would look up, see his name on the sign, and go to the phone.

One evening I was in the bar at the Europa with some ABC News colleagues when we heard the bell and the bellman's voice ring out: "Mr. C-Ten-F-F-Eye" — he punctuated the name with two rings of the bell — "Paging Mr. C-Ten-F-F-Eye."

"With a name like that, the guy must be a spy," I said to my friends.

No one answered the page in the lobby area, so the bellman walked up to the bar where we were sitting and repeated his call for that "Mr. C-Ten-F-F-Eye."

Then we saw the sign, and my colleague, correspondent Lou Cioffi, jumped up to go to the phone, followed by our hoots of laughter.

. ON *the* LIGHT SIDE

OOPS

Live television is fun. It's real. It's invigorating. It is also a part of our business that creates some memorable and humiliating moments. For example . . .

The Hawks had played (and lost) a game in Philadelphia's Spectrum. At game's end, during the commercial break, I took off my headset and turned to face the camera so we could do the close "On Camera." The commercial ended, the man pointed, the red light went on, and I began to talk. Behind the camera people were waving at me, swearing at me, doing totally weird things. I stop and say, "Is something wrong?" Finally the A.D. says, "Pick up your hand-held." I had managed to take off the headpiece mike but neglected to pick up the other one. Somewhat abashed, I held up the mike, explained to the viewers what it did, and guaranteed them that I knew all the time and just wanted to prove to them how important these microphones are.

■ ■ ■

I was doing a postgame show in Shea Stadium after a Braves loss. Preston Hanna had pitched well for Atlanta, striking out a lot of guys, but he made a fielding error that wound up costing him and his team the game. Preston obligingly went on the postgame show with me, and I, ever the diplomat, cut immediately to

Skip working a Hawks game in the late '70s. (Courtesy the Atlanta Journal-Constitution*)*

the chase. "Preston, you pitched a heckuva ballgame, but you were the architect of your own destruction with that bad throw to the plate. What happened on that play?" Preston gazed steadfastly at the camera and responded, "Well, Skip, the ball was hit right back to me. I was going to go to second and try to get a double play, but I sort of slipped . . . and then I decided to try for the guy at home and I threw off balance . . . and . . . awww, bottom line is I just made a horseshit play." I thanked Preston for his keen insight on the day's events and retreated with him to the clubhouse for a cold one I felt we both richly deserved.

■ ■ ■

I was doing color commentary while my dear friend Ernie Johnson was doing the play-by-play. Mike Schmidt is hitting and Rick Mahler is pitching. On the air it sounded something like this:

EJ: "Mahler delivers. It's a change of pace. Schmidt hits a high drive to left. Gary Matthews goes back and makes the catch."

SC (looking at slow-motion replay): "Well, Ernie, as you can see, Mahler had him completely off-stride on that pitch. He was so fooled, he had only one hand on the bat when he swung. And still, he hit it to the warning track in deep left center. The moral of the story is . . . boy, that shit sure is strong."

No, I didn't pause. When something like that happens the best thing to do is to keep on blabbering so that people will *think* that they misheard rather than that you misspoke. I talked for perhaps twenty seconds about what a nice night it was; how well Mahler was pitching; that the Mets would follow the Phils into town for a big weekend series. At no time did I laugh. I pulled it off. I nodded to Ernie who said. "Here's Gary Maddux to hit. And the first pitch is a curveball over the outside corner for a strike. Skip, what's the name of their third baseman again?"

We both went up like skyrockets. All anybody heard for the rest of that inning was two supposed adults giggling like teenagers. For the rest of his great career, whenever Mike came to the plate against Atlanta and I was on the air, it was, "Here's the Phillies hall of famer . . ." or "here's Mike . . ." or "here's the power-hitting third-sacker." I had gotten into deep Schmidt with his name once. I didn't want to do it again.

■ ■ ■

I was working a radio game with Ernie in the bad old days when the Braves were almost always terrible, and this night was no exception. We were getting hammered something like 14-1 before a crowd of about 2,500. One of the few bright spots of the season was outfielder Jeff Burroughs, who had a big year for us, hitting more than forty home runs. Some of his fans had taken to bringing a banner to the park each night which said JEFF'S JOINT and was displayed in the right field area where Burroughs patrolled.

Ernie was doing play-by-play, and I was just sitting there, doing nothing. Like the crowd, I had been induced into a near trance-like lethargy by the play of our local heroes. Imagine my shock, then, when I heard Ernie say, "Well, I see that Jeff's joint is out tonight." I fell immediately to the floor and burst into hysterical laughter. Ernie had no idea what he had said. I knew what he *meant*, and I knew what he *said*, and that made it even funnier. Too bad nobody was listening.

■ ■ ■

I believe it was at Cobo Arena where I was televising a game in which the Hawks played the Detroit Pistons. There I am with the best seat in the house — a heavy table right at courtside. I'm working alone and a loose ball heads my way, followed by several players. One of them, Detroit's John Mengeldt, dives into the table to try to keep the ball in play. I try to get up to knock him back into the court, and I'm halfway there when the table hits me right in the groin. A tip to young broadcasters: broadcasting in this condition is no fun. For the entire second quarter I sounded like Maria Callas.

■ ■ ■

Talking about the new female public address announcer in San Francisco and being ever mindful of the women's rights movement, I tried to be complimentary. I said, "Well, I gotta tell you, it's going to take some getting used to. But at least she's not a screamer like some of these guys." My partner, Don Sutton, vacated the booth with alacrity, allowing me to attempt to extricate myself from a very deep chasm. All I could say was, "You know, I probably could have phrased that better," and plowed on.

■ ■ ■

We get lots of cards and letters from fans, and when the opportunity presents itself, we try to acknowledge a few of them on the air. Pete mentioned that some fans were looking in from the Virgin Islands. Without thinking, as usual, I replied, "I wonder how those islands got their name? Must be a pretty good story." Pete then left the booth. (That happens to me a lot.)

■   ■   ■

One day when I was working alone in Los Angeles, we came back from a break with a shot of a beautiful girl about to eat a hotdog. Being from LA, she knew when the camera was on her, and she played to the audience, doing to that hotdog what I can only leave to your imagination. There are times when even I know there is nothing to be said. From director Tom Smith, in my headpiece I hear, "Jesus Christ, that bitch just got me fired." It wasn't Smitty's fault. That's live television.

■   ■   ■

Another time in the City of Angels and again with Smitty at the helm, the Dodgers held a Business Persons Special. As it turned out, some of the business persons were from what some say is the world's oldest business. The unfortunate Smith got a shot of some of these young ladies just as they decided to moon the camera. It was not necessarily a pretty sight, but as Smitty cut away, I couldn't help but say, "We feel like a bunch of tardy butchers here. We apologize for getting a little behind in our work." Smitty was, of course, inconsolable.

■   ■   ■

An announcer who shall remain nameless was once broadcasting a day game in San Francisco. He broadcast for a team in the East, and his team was ahead by something like 9-2. Glancing at his watch the announcer excitedly proclaimed, "It's 9-2 here in the eighth, and it's just five till four here local time. Why, we'll be out of here in time to savor the fruits of this fine city."

His partner said nothing, took off his headphones, put down his microphone, walked out of the booth, and collapsed in laughter in the hallway outside.

THE EAGLE HAS LANDED — TAPE AT ELEVEN

The phone rang at my home, near the ABC News bureau in Atlanta, about 11:15 a.m. on Sunday, July 20, 1969.

Neil Armstrong was scheduled to land on the moon at 4:18 p.m. that day and then actually step onto the moon's surface later that night. A producer at ABC Radio News in New York had a brilliant notion as to what the Atlanta bureau should do to help cover it.

"Hey Don, great idea here. We want you to go to downtown Atlanta and get the reaction of people on the street to the moon landing," he said. He was so full of enthusiasm that you'd have thought he just discovered a sure cure for the cold.

"Well, Walt," I said, "isn't the moon landing set for about eleven o'clock tonight?"

"Sure is, and we want some good reax from R.P.s." (Translation: Reaction from "real people," as opposed to politicians or celebrities.)

"Well, Walt," I responded, "anybody on the streets of downtown Atlanta at 11:00 p.m. on a Sunday is not somebody you'd want to hear from."

"Hey, we're doing it all over the country and we need Southern reax," he said.

"Walt, believe me, the only people on the streets here at that hour probably would be a lot more likely to steal my tape recorder than talk into it."

He was quiet for a second, then said, "Well, OK then, just go around your neighborhood or some other residential area and get reax."

"Hey, Walt, you know what'll happen if I go knocking on doors around here at that hour on Sunday night? The sound you hear on the tape will be a shotgun blast and my agonized screaming," I explained.

"Why is that?" Walt asked.

"Because anybody banging on doors at that hour will wake up some guy with a gun under his bed who'll think that the urban hordes have come to the suburbs to kill his family and appropriate his riding lawn mower," I said.

"Well, you gotta get some R.P. reax as soon as they land and feed it to us for tomorrow morning's newscasts," he said. "You gotta do it," he repeated, and hung up.

So I threw a party. I invited to my house everybody I knew who might be able to make a cogent comment about history in the making after a few drinks late on a Sunday night.

My first thought in that regard was Skip Caray, my old friend who at the time was the announcer for the Atlanta Hawks of the NBA.

"What time did you say you wanted us for this party?" he asked when I called him.

"Oh, we'll start about nine-thirty, watch Neil Armstrong step on the moon about eleven, then have some food and that'll do it."

"Neil Armstrong . . . Neil Armstrong," Skip muttered. "Is he a point guard or what?" he asked.

That was Skip's idea of a joke on himself and other sports announcers. Or, in retrospect, it may have been his joke on those of us in TV news, who he claimed wouldn't know a point guard from a security guard.

Skip was no stranger to partying at midnight, but he usually started earlier. I also invited some other ABC News colleagues and most of my neighbors. They probably figured that if they did me that favor, they could borrow my deluxe suburban car-washing hose accessory for about a year.

The moon landing was a success, you'll recall. Armstrong put his left foot on the surface of the moon at exactly 10:56:19 p.m. The party turned out OK too.

I got out my tape recorder, went around and interviewed everybody, getting their "real people" reactions to the moon landing. When I called New York to feed the tape, the producer was ecstatic.

"Great stuff, man. How'd you get it?"

"Well, Walt, I know the South, ya know, and I know where to go to get what I need," I answered, standing in my own bedroom, using the phone on the bedside table. He had no idea that all those "real people" were my party guests, nor that I would put the party on my expense account.

"All those people, so happy about the moon landing," he said.

"They sounded so excited they could hardly talk," he gushed.

He never knew that some of my friends could hardly talk because they were up way past their Sunday night bedtimes and had had about eight drinks before that "one giant step for mankind."

Walt was curious about one of the interviews.

"Who was that nut who claimed that he gave NASA that line for Armstrong — 'one small step for man'?" Walt asked.

"Oh, ignore that. It was just some wacko who wandered by," I said, realizing that I had forgotten to erase Skip's contribution to my historic coverage of the moon landing, as experienced in the suburbs of Atlanta.

BAR WARS

After a night game in Pittsburgh, I was sitting at a booth in the hotel lounge with traveling secretary Bill Acree and the late, great pitching coach and former major league catcher Rube Walker. We were sharing our hotel with a large contingent of Shriners who were working out of the Pittsburgh Arena right across the street. Also in the saloon was my friend and partner John Sterling. John, then a bachelor, was with a very lovely young lady at the bar. He nodded toward the three of us and said, "send those clowns a drink." The bartender did. John's Bill was $147.50. He had bought a drink for us and every clown-attired Shriner in the room.

■ ■ ■

Anyone who has ever watched the Braves/Hawks on TV knows I have a constant (and mostly losing) battle with my weight. I am living proof that the phrase "just another pretty face" isn't always the rule in our business. One time those weight battles almost got me in deep trouble. I had been put on diuretic pills by a doctor of somewhat dubious reputation. The Hawks were about to take on Kareem and the Lakers at the Georgia Tech coliseum where the Hawks first played their games in Atlanta. I should point out that the building is a sunken pit and once you reach the floor, you are a long way away from any kind of privacy.

As was my custom in those days, I stopped with my sportswriter buddy Frank Hyland for a pregame pick-me-up — a cocktail or two. Frank's dad, a retired Army colonel, was in town, and we began listening to his fascinating war stories. We also upped our consumption. Roughly an hour before game time, I rushed into the coliseum to do the pregame show and get ready for the game. I had time to do little else, but in those days my bladder was the best in the business. Of course I forgot about the diuretics I had just started taking. I began to notice some discomfort at halftime, but because I had gotten to the gym so late, I hadn't taped anything. And since I worked alone, I had to conduct the halftime interview live.

By the end of the third quarter I was in considerable pain, but I figured I could handle it. And I would have, too, but some jerk hit a last-second basket to send us into overtime. By now, the only word to describe my situation was agony. Then we went to a second overtime period. My definition of poise? Being able to urinate into a used Coke cup under a press table while eight thousand people watch Kareem Abdul Jabbar make a hookshot and your statistician is in hysterics.

I'm afraid I left the full cup under the table after the game. I hope the clean-up crew didn't think someone had forgotten their beer.

■ ■ ■

Former Braves catcher Bruce Benedict was a funny kid and a courageous one, too. He took a hit from Steve Garvey one night on a play at the plate that literally could have killed him. But he held onto the ball and got the out.

Bruce and I crossed paths one night after a game, and what started out as "maybe just one" cocktail turned into quite a few for both of us. We had a day game in Cincinnati the next day — a 12:30 Business Persons Special. Benedict and I had very little sleep, but that was the norm for me and it didn't appear a problem for Bruce either. A righthander was supposed to pitch for the Reds, and Joe Nolan was scheduled to do the catching for us. It was 94 degrees when I waddled into the dugout before the game and was confronted by an ashen-faced Benedict. "Look at the bleeping lineup card," he said. I looked. The Reds had changed to a lefty, and Benedict was penciled in behind the plate. I started laughing and so did he.

When I got to the booth, he was running in the outfield trying to sweat out quite a few cold ones. When he saw me watching and laughing, he sprawled in mid-stride to the ground, spread-eagled as if dead. Thirty thousand people thought he was crazy. Had they only known. He got a hit, by the way, but we got beat as usual.

EAR-TO-MOUTH RESUSCI-TATION

Skip and I were talking about the routine nature of our jobs one night when we discovered we had something in common. We both had been doing TV long enough to be able to switch to automatic pilot when necessary.

In Skip's case, it has to do with announcing basketball, which he has done for so long that it has become second nature to describe the action, fast as it is.

"It's a skill that some people have," he explained. "I realized after I had been doing Atlanta Hawks games on radio for many years, that I could do the play-by-play of the game and balance my checkbook at the same time."

He exaggerates to make the point, but Skip has the wonderful knack of being able to see something happening in front of him and to describe it so vividly that the listener might as well be right there with him. He wasn't bragging about it; it's just something that some people can do.

In news, we don't often have that "play-by-play" situation to deal with. Our rote reporting is more often a matter of reading a news story off the TelePrompTer. Sometimes, if I know the story well or have written it myself, I can read the story off the prompter with feeling, or at least with meaning, and be thinking of something entirely different.

Which is not to say that I am indifferent to the story I am reading, or that Skip isn't interested in the game he's describing. It's just a necessary tool of the trade.

Some television reporters who do broadcasts from the field use another technique, usually called the "ear prompter." It is the mechanical equivalent of reading *this* and thinking about *that*.

It came in especially handy while I was covering the U.S. Congress, where I had to do "standups," live reports in front of the Capitol. It's tough to memorize forty-five seconds or a minute of copy, so I would write the script, then record it on a small, mini-cassette audio recorder. I would then plug an earpiece into the recorder and run it up my suitcoat, out of my collar and into my ear.

When I got my cue, I would turn on the little recorder, hear my own voice reading the script, look earnestly into the TV camera, and then just repeat what I heard in my ear. Many of us did that; many network reporters still do. Once you learn to listen and repeat a half-second after yourself, you can do a minute or more that way and make it seem as though you really know your stuff.

Of course you pray that the batteries don't go bad at a crucial point in your live report. You also pray that Phil Jones of CBS News is nowhere around.

Phil is one of the smartest reporters in Washington. He's on the "48 Hours" program for CBS News now, but was a wizard at covering Congress when I was doing the same for ABC News.

Phil also covered the White House once in a while. One day he was working in the press room there and saw ABC News correspondent Ann Compton go out to the White House lawn to do a live report. Knowing that Ann used the "ear prompter" technique, Phil sneaked up behind her, then got on the ground and crept to where she was standing, the recorder in her hand behind her back.

As Ann was talking, repeating on camera what she had recorded moments before, Phil reached up, just out of camera range, and pulled the earpiece cord out of the earplug jack. Phil then crept backward, stood up, and jogged back to the press room, laughing hysterically.

But the laugh was on him. Ann heard her voice stop, so she stopped. But she's a pro and knew her material, so the audience never knew there was anything wrong. She finished her report, signed off, and spent the next week or so trying to think of a way to retaliate.

She probably thought of several outrageous acts of revenge, but Ann Compton is a very nice person. As far as I know, she never really nailed him for that. Still, it's only been about fifteen years, so Phil Jones, wherever you are, watch out.

BARING
ALL IN
MONTREAL

Of all the dumb things I have done in my life, the dumbest and potentially most damaging occurred in the lovely city of Montreal. It was back in the '70s when the team was terrible, attendance was worse, and in those days the Braves flew mostly on commercial airliners. We played a Thursday night game in Atlanta and, as usual, it was a nightmare. The final score was something like 15-5 against — and the game seemed like it took thirty-two hours.

We left the ballpark around 11:45 p.m. after the postgame shows, arrived home at 12:30 a.m., and got to sleep at about 1:00 a.m. We were booked on a 9:00 a.m. flight to Montreal through Boston the next day, which meant arising at 6:30 a.m. and fighting traffic to get to the ballpark at 7:30 a.m. and take the bus to the airport. I made it in good shape, but the flight was an hour late leaving Atlanta, and there was another hour delay in Boston. By the time we got to the hotel, we had just thirty minutes before we headed to the brand new Olympic Stadium for the game. The results: another huge loss and another game of a good deal more than three hours.

The bus didn't leave for forty-five minutes after the game, and it was an exhausted group that sailed through the lobby of the La Cite hotel. Everybody headed straight for the sack and some sleep. Everybody, that is, except for Pete Van Wieren and myself, who decided to have "just one" nightcap before retiring for the evening. One turned into something like five and it was about

3:00 a.m. when we headed for our rooms. I undressed, neatly hung up my clothes — all of my clothes — and went to bed. I slept like a log until 6:00 a.m. when I felt the need to urinate. Still at least half asleep, I did my duty, washed my hands, staggered out of the bathroom and did what I do at home in similar situations: turn right. I opened the door and heard a little click as I moved toward what I thought was my bed. The click was the sound of the hotel door slamming behind me. There I was — large, nude, and suddenly wide awake — in the hotel corridor of the good old La Cite.

My first thought was, "My God, I'm not even in my own country." My second thought was that at any moment an elderly couple would leave their room on my floor (the 8th) of the hotel and the sight of me (not pretty even at the best of times) would cause one or both of them to suffer a coronary. I tried the door about fifty times, begging it to open. No such luck. Still undetected, I raced down the hall (picture that in your mind's eye) and found a linen closet. I leaped inside, figuring I could wrap a sheet around me and go to the lobby. It would be humiliating, but I wouldn't be arrested for indecent exposure. I picked a linen closet that had no linens, but it did have a telephone. Even better. I would call my partner in crime, Van Wieren, and he would go get a key for me. Pete was tired too. His phone rang at least a hundred times and he slept right through it.

Desperately, I dialed Wayne Minshew, at the time the beat writer for the *Atlanta Constitution*. He awakened after five rings. "What room are you in?" says I. "842," says he. What luck. "Open your door. I'll be right there," says I. I get to his room and I slip inside. Minshew is still half asleep. "Wayne, please go to the lobby and get me a key to 812." He dresses and departs, and I tie a towel (okay, it took two towels) around my waist.

Minshew returns with my key. I peek out the door. The coast is clear. I race back to my room, open the door, and collapse in hilarious laughter. I must have laughed at myself for an hour before I finally fell asleep. I slept so well that I missed the team bus for the Saturday afternoon game at the Olympic Stadium. No problem. Montreal has a great subway system called the Metro, and I hop aboard headed for the ballpark.

Suddenly a familiar voice from across the aisle chirps, "Hello there, sleepy head." It's the dapper Van Wieren, well rested and ready to go. He was nonplused when I called him a "deaf *&¢%$*&#." Then I told him the story. Why not? By now Minshew would have told the world anyway. Pete laughed so hard that everyone in our car was staring at him. When we got to the Stadium, we parted company. I headed for the pressbox and a much needed cup of coffee while Pete went directly to the field to tape the "award winning" pregame show.

As I sipped my coffee and gazed down at the field, I saw Van Wieren in the dugout talking to a couple of players. Soon, more players gathered around him, and it wasn't long before our entire team and about half the Expos were crowding in. Van Wieren was like Radio Free Europe telling my sad tale.

To make it worse, Minshew strolls up to the booth and says, "I wonder if I need psychiatric help?" I ask him what he means. He replies, "I had the strangest dream of my life last night and it concerned you." It was no gag. Wayne, God love him, really had thought the whole thing was a dream. And, thinking it a dream, he was a good deal concerned about trying to interpret it. I started laughing all over again, went to the field to face the music, and first ran into our leftfielder Gary Mathews.

As other players swarmed toward me, Mathews said, "Skip, why didn't you take your key?" To which I replied, "Gary, that's the difference between black guys and white guys. White guys don't take their keys to pee at 6:00 a.m." I've never lived it down. Players I had never met came up to me for years asking if the story was true. It was. Incidentally, I think we lost that Saturday game 16-6.

CHICKEN

NOODLE

NEWS

CNN needs no praise from me these days. Everyone knows it is a world-class operation now. That was not always true.

The traditional TV networks snickered a lot at CNN in its early days, so Chris and I were among the snickerees, having joined CNN a couple of months before it went on the air. We didn't need the derision of the other broadcasters in those early days. We saw enough and took part in enough silliness at CNN to keep ourselves in stitches.

One day in 1981, we were anchoring our midday program when a major overhead light exploded right above us. The smoking remnants of the light fell between us, right into a wastebasket. Viewers could see the flaming debris plummet past us. Within a few seconds the smoldering pieces had ignited the papers and other trash in the wastebasket, and the smoke and flames flickered up between us.

We looked at each other and decided not to ignore it.

"Well, we have a problem here; the wastebasket is on fire," said one of us — I can't remember who.

I beckoned to the floor manager, a young woman just beginning her career at CNN, and signaled her to remove the wastebasket. She looked worried but refused to budge. The flames grew, the smoke spread, but everyone seemed paralyzed by the burning basket.

I think we went to a commercial break about then, and a technician ran up to the set, doused the fire, and removed the smelly, smoking basket. Later, the young floor director told us that she didn't come get the fire off the set because one of her trainers told her that she should never, ever walk in front of a hot camera.

Rules are rules.

■ ■ ■

One of CNN's early weathercasters was Stuart Saroka. He wasn't there very long, perhaps because his first day on the job was a tough one.

At that time, CNN had a peculiar, round set that was supposed to revolve, but which never really worked without the pushing and shoving of several strong men. One third of that immovable revolving set was dedicated to weather. On it was a weather board divided into vertical segments that would each turn 180 degrees with the push of a button, to change the visual display.

Picture vertical blinds. When you pull the chain, each strip changes from back to front. You get the idea.

On Saroka's first day at CNN, while doing his inaugural weathercast, he pushed the button for the weather board to do its flip-flop. Nothing. Nothing moved. Saroka pushed again, harder, and when that didn't work, he stuck his hand between two of the strips and tugged.

The boards gave a little, moved a bit, and Saroka's hand slipped further into the abyss. He pushed harder, still jabbering to the audience about high pressure or whatever. The boards then jumped, moved, and swung back to their original position, pinning Saroka at about his elbow. The more he struggled, the deeper his arm went.

By the time he was trapped up to his shoulder, he gave up the pretense of continuing his weather report and shouted, on the air, to news anchorman Dave Walker, "Dave, help me!"

I honestly cannot recall now whether Saroka outlasted that soon-to-be-ash-canned weather board. Neither was there very long, but both will long be remembered.

■   ■   ■

CNN's best of all weathercasters, in my view, was and is Flip Spiceland. He is one of those broadcast pros who takes his job seriously but not himself.

One of Flip's favorite CNN moments was in 1982. He was doing a routine weather report in the early afternoon: ". . . and so for the Southeast, the forecast for tonight is . . ." At that second, all the lights went out in the CNN studio.

What the viewer saw was total blackness on the screen. What the viewer heard was Flip, pausing only slightly before continuing his report: ". . . the forecast for tonight is, uh, dark, very dark. Yes I can tell you it is gonna be real dark . . ."

That CNN moment ended up on one of those TV blooper shows on one of the networks. Flip got paid a couple hundred dollars for its use. Then it was sold to a cable network, then to some foreign stations. Every time somebody aired the tape of Flip telling CNN viewers that the forecast for that night was "dark, real dark," he got another check in the mail. By the time the checks stopped coming, Flip had made about $1500 extra dollars, for just doing his job — that is, looking around at his environment and reporting his observations.

■ ■ ■

One day shortly before Christmas in 1982, our anchor colleague Kathleen Sullivan stopped by our little office at CNN with a piece of news copy in her hand.

"Look at this," she said, waving the paper at me. "Is this a joke or are they serious about me reading this on the air?"

She wasn't laughing, so I looked at the script. It was a story that would touch a lot of hearts during that holiday season. Seems a little boy named Johnny had been born with a congenital heart defect. By the age of five or so, Johnny already had endured something like twenty-three major heart surgeries. But a recent operation finally had fixed Johnny's problem.

The story detailed how Johnny's loving family would be able to take him home from the hospital in time for Christmas. The last paragraph, the one that had Kathleen worried, read: "So this year, for the first time, Johnny's Mommy and Daddy will be able to open their presents at Christmas, instead of opening Johnny."

I laughed, assuming it was some writer's twisted idea of holiday humor.

"I'm not reading this," Kathleen said. "Would you read this?" she asked us.

I shook my head, and she said, "Well, I'm not either, and that's that."

Kathleen Sullivan went on to ABC and CBS and those lose-weight commercials, but she may never have done a greater service to TV viewers than she did that day way back when at CNN, when she decided not to read the last paragraph of the story about a kid named Johnny.

Come to think of it, had she read it as written, the embarrassment might have kept us shackled with that "Chicken Noodle News" label a little longer.

A PORTRAIT GALLERY

THE

JIGGS

IS UP

Those of us who are fortunate in life meet at least one really good friend. I've been blessed with several, but right at the top of the heap is John Kenneth "Jiggs" McDonald, now the voice of the New York Islanders and once the voice of the now-defunct Atlanta Flames.

That Jiggs and I became friends at all is a bit of an oddity. Atlanta's indoor arena, the Omni, had just been completed, and the Flames had been formed to share the space with the Hawks, who were moving over from Georgia Tech. Basketball had met with only moderate success, and there was fear in the Hawks' front office that the Flames would be our death knell. Nobody knew how hockey would go over in the South, so the Flames people were a little leery about us too.

A cocktail party was thrown for the staff of the building, both teams, and the high-rollers who could afford season tickets. It was held right on the floor of the Omni itself. McDonald and I had never met, but he was aware of who I was and I of him. We were like two prize fighters circling one another in the first round. Finally, after a couple of glasses of the bubbly, the whole thing began to strike me as silly. Finally I walked up to him and said, "Look, you know who I am and I know who you are. The hell with these people. Let's be friends until one of us does something to screw it up."

Twenty-five years later we still haven't screwed it up. Instead of fighting, we both became ambassadors for the other's team. We even wound up with a talk show together, for which we got paid almost nothing and for which the ratings were phenomenal. If you had that show in Atlanta today we both would have made six figures from it alone. Our friendship was based, of course, on the needle.

Jiggs is short in stature and prone to weight. I am taller and also prone to weight. It started with fat jokes and soon escalated. Jiggs has always blamed me for instigating what became near-guerrilla warfare. It seems that on one of his birthdays, several tons of chicken manure mysteriously found their way onto his driveway. How he could blame two outstanding citizens like Boom Boom

Geoffrion and myself for such a caper is hard to fathom. But, having no imagination, he resorted to the same childish prank on my birthday and went so far as to have the TBS Sports crew on hand, cameras rolling, when he dumped unprocessed chicken manure on my driveway. When it's unprocessed, you can't spread it because it will kill your grass and shrubs. Obviously, too, Jiggs had stayed up all night feeding these particular chickens lasagna or something. The stench was overpowering.

Unfazed, I immediately went on the air the next day and announced that I had several tons of unprocessed chicken manure that I was giving away. I gave the number at the Braves' switchboard, which was immediately overloaded. The first guy to get there was told to haul it off — but to leave one very small pile next to the driveway.

The next evening wife Paula and I dressed in dark clothes (our very best ninja outfits) and headed under cover of darkness to the McDonalds' palatial estate out in Marietta. We were accompanied by the remaining manure. I stuffed his mailbox with most of the stuff, placed the rest in a paper bag and lit it, then rang his doorbell. The poor dingbat stomped it out. As soon as his olfactory glands began working he realized what had befallen him, much to the delight of his wonderful wife, Marilyn. We entered the house and partied till very late in the evening — so late, in fact, that McDonald overslept. But Marilyn awoke right on time and went out to get her hubby the paper, which, in Marietta, is placed in one's mailbox. Marilyn returned to the house with a little more than all the news that was fit to print, and the McDonalds immediately began plotting revenge.

It took a year but victory was theirs. Paula threw a birthday party for me and invited a bunch of friends. All were kind enough to bring gifts, including Jiggs and Marilyn. Their gift, however, came in the form of a live adult goat, complete with a sign reading, "Happy birthday, you old goat." The goat went nuts when he saw our Airedale and our Lab. They went nuts when they saw him. The neighbor's German shepherd went crazy, as did the collie across the street. By the time we got the goat back to the goat farm, two Fulton County police cruisers had seen fit to stop by and see what the disturbance was all about. You have never seen policemen laugh so hard. The little devil beat me fair and square.

It was a deeper friendship than just fun and games. Jiggs was the best man at my wedding to Paula — the biggest honor I could think to bestow upon him.

Jiggs once asked an interesting favor of me. The Flames by then were in terrible financial trouble. The National Hockey League had lost its television contract, the World Hockey Association had started driving players' salaries through the roof, and after a rous-ing initial success the Flames' fortunes were in decline as well. Money was tight for the franchise and a little tight for Jiggs. But because of his tremendous talent, the folks at "Hockey Night" in Canada called him and asked him to do some games for them. Some of those games conflicted with the Flames' schedule. His bosses said they would let him go but that he would have to pay for a replacement announcer. In desperation he turned to me — a guy who had seen maybe ten hockey matches in my life. It was important to him, so I said I would do it. Anything for a friend and all that — but I was scared to death.

I went to a couple of games and tried to broadcast them in my head, but it was a terrible mess. I kept screwing up the names. I had no problem with the Flames guys. They were fellas I had run the streets with before my marriage to Paula. But I didn't know enough about hockey to get the other team straight in my head. I drove toward the Omni for my first hockey match with fear in my heart.

Suddenly, inspired by panic, a brilliant idea hit me. If I didn't know who played for the bleeping Toronto Maple Leafs, there was a good chance that a large majority of the listening audience didn't know either. The Leafs in those days had one really good player — #8, Lanny McDonald. I just memorized him and made up the names for everybody else. I used high school football teammates and college fraternity brothers to round out that Toronto team. When-ever anyone shot at the goal, I would merely say, "He shoots . . ." and if it missed I'd follow with, "Don Farmer's shot went wide." If he scored I'd say, "He scores!" Then I'd look at their roster and come up with the proper name.

I didn't know how it had actually worked until I headed (as fast as possible) to the Omni Club after the game. The Omni Club was a place where the seasoned hockey fans gathered after the game to review that night's play. Many of them, in fact, got to the Omni Club after the first period and never made it back to their seats, relying instead on the play-by-play announcer to keep them up on the action. The place was packed by the time I got there, and my appearance prompted an ovation from people telling me I was "almost as good as Jiggs."

I did a couple more games for him that year, fortunately against obscure teams, and my ruse worked in all of them. My bio still says I broadcast National Hockey League games, and I laugh every time I see it. The only person who laughed harder than me was my friend Jiggs when I came clean on what I had done.

Speaking of faking it, he and I did that together when the powers that be at the Omni decided to stage the first ever indoor soccer game played in North America. It was between a bunch of U.S. soccer pros and the Hungarian National Team. We had never broadcast soccer, had no idea what indoor soccer was all about, and didn't really give a bleep about it either. All I remember is that the Hungarian team had more "koffs" than a military doctor and the final score was 9-8. I honestly don't remember who won.

When the Flames left for Calgary, Jiggs left for the Island. I miss him to this day and, every now and then, I find myself driving by that house in Marietta just to remember the fun that we had. There was nobody more devastated by the McDonalds' leaving town than the Carays, except for the McDonalds.

GEORGE

FOR

PRESIDENT

I have covered more presidential candidates than most reporters, and most of the men I covered lost. I did cover George Bush, once, but it was the time he lost the nomination to Ronald Reagan. When he won the presidency, somebody else covered him.

Coincidentally, I've covered several other candidates who were named George. My first George was Romney, the governor of Michigan who wanted to be president. Thatch of steel-gray hair, steely stare, crooked smile but straight teeth, Romney had the look of a leader. Then one day he made that offhand remark about Vietnam, that he had been "brainwashed" about the war, and he was done.

Romney didn't like reporters much, but once he invited all of us who covered his presidential effort and our spouses to a weekend of fun at Mackinac Island, on Michigan's upper peninsula. It's a nice place, and the Governor and his wife were charming hosts. Their Mormon faith prohibits using alcohol, but they made it available to their guests, knowing that reporters don't stay long in booze-free zones.

On Saturday night, the Romneys hosted a dinner at the Inn there. On my left at the table was Bill Stout, a CBS News correspondent. On his left was Don Oliver from NBC News. We all enjoyed the evening and the drinks and wine that flowed freely, but Bill Stout was having an especially good time.

After the meal, Romney and his wife stood up and welcomed everyone. Stout had been designated ahead of time to speak for all of us, with a quick thanks for the weekend. Trouble was, Stout was drunk. He also didn't like the Romneys much.

He stood, went to the microphone, belched a small belch and stared at the Romneys. They were seated now, staring back at Bill with some contempt for his inebriated state. As reporters, wives, state officials, campaign workers, and the Romneys looked on, Bill said: "I just have one thing to say to Governor Romney tonight. Governor, up yours."

Don listens as presidential candidate George Bush makes a point.

Don Oliver and I jumped up, went to the microphone, took Stout by the elbows, and guided him out of the room.

Governor Romney eventually revived his own pulse, stood up, and said with some grace, "I think Mr. Stout has enjoyed himself a little too much tonight, so let's go on with the party . . ."

Romney didn't appear to have gotten mad. But he did get even. Late that night, something came up in the Romney campaign that required him to change plans and leave the island early the next day for an event out of state. Romney's people alerted all of us about the early flight — all of us but Bill Stout.

We didn't know until later that Stout slept until about noon the next day, then awoke to find that Romney and the traveling press corps had left hours earlier. Stout had some explaining to do to CBS News. The Romney press people said it was an oversight and they were sorry.

WHEN GEORGE McGOVERN DECIDED to run against President Nixon in 1972, ABC News assigned me to cover the McGovern campaign. At that point, I was the only network correspondent so assigned, so I got to ride around with McGovern in small, chartered planes to a lot of small towns. He was a nice guy, but with all the other Democrats clamoring for the chance to run against Mr. Nixon that year, I never thought McGovern would have a chance for the nomination. After days of tracking his low-budget visits to New Hampshire and other early primary states, I was tired of what seemed to be a non-story. So I jumped at the chance to be assigned to the ABC News London Bureau in early February, rather than stay with the McGovern campaign.

Shortly after Chris and I got married and moved to Europe, McGovern emerged as the Democrats' front-runner. Later, of course, he was wiped out in the general election, so I made the right choice. England is, after all, forever.

■ ■ ■

Before the McGovern "George" and after the Romney one came the Wallace one — George Wallace, the feisty, nasty governor of Alabama who attracted a lot of support, not only because of his racism, but because of his "everyman" approach, his view of most other politicians as "pointy-headed intellectuals" who were out of touch with real America. Covering Wallace gave me a real dose of his "real America."

Wallace loved to make speeches in school or church auditoriums, where he would be up on stage, with the audience below him in chairs and us TV guys bunched down in front of the stage. The governor would use us as bait, to stir up his crowds. Here's how it went, on many occasions:

"My friends, there's not a dime's worth of difference between these other so-called leaders," he would say, and the crowd would roar.

"And my friends, those liberal, fellow-traveler newsmen are the worst of all. They come down here from Neeew Yorrrk Citeh, tellin' lies about us and our people, stirring up trouble . . ."

As he continued to deride us journalists, the people in the auditorium would turn their noisy anger on us, shouting, salivating, shaking their fists.

"They show what they want to show on TV every night, makin' folks up North think we're full of hate. Well, we don't hate anybody, except maybe these *news* people," Wallace would say, drawing the word out contemptuously.

By now the audience would be in a frenzy, shouting insults at the two or three network news reporters and cameramen who were recording the event. We would turn cameras and lights to the crowd, and they would go mad with anger and indignation.

It got pretty scary, with Wallace up there pounding on the podium about the evil journalists that had impugned the integrity of Dixie. Then, when it seemed that the crowd would attack us physically any second, Wallace would thrust his hand in the air, palm out and say:

"Now wait a minute, don't be messin' with these boys down here in front. They alright, they with me."

That would freeze the troublemakers for a second. Could they believe what they heard, that their hero didn't want them to beat up these "long-haired Yankee TV guys"?

And Wallace then would repeat his praise for us: "These boys have been covering me for awhile, and I know 'em. I even like 'em a little.

"It's their pointy-headed bosses in Neew Yawk that's the problem. So y'all be nice to my boys; they makin' me famous and your next president!!!" (His exclamation points.)

That calmed the crowd enough for us to pack up and get out before the real troublemakers could rekindle their violent instincts and crease our skulls with an axe handle.

■   ■   ■

Some non-Georges also are on the list of would-be presidents I covered and watched fail. They include Birch Bayh, Walter Mondale (although he did win the vice-presidency), Henry "Scoop" Jackson, Howard Baker, Hubert Humphrey, Barry Goldwater, Eugene McCarthy, Richard Nixon — no, he won, didn't he.

And Gerald Ford, of course. He got the job without running for it and lost when he ran for it. I'm not sure how that affects my won-lost record.

One of the most decent people ever to enter politics was Morris K. Udall, the Congressman from Arizona who ran for president in 1976.

He was "Mo" to his family and friends and to many of us in the traveling press corps who covered him. Udall was a witty, urbane, mostly honest politician. That made it obvious to those of us who liked him and covered him that he had no chance at all to win the nomination. Sometimes the press corps would save Udall from himself, not unlike the way reporters often helped Barry Goldwater out of verbal jams.

The joke in the press corps when Goldwater ran for president in 1964 was that all the reporters had a special key installed on their typewriters. When pressed, that key would punch out, in any story quoting Goldwater, this line: "Later, an aide explained that what Senator Goldwater meant to say was . . ."

With Udall, we didn't need that sort of preset keyboard, but we sometimes just didn't bother to report his witticisms.

The one that sticks in my mind came on a dreary day on the campaign bus. We had just landed at the airport in Cleveland and were busing to a campaign stop downtown. As the bus approached the city, Udall looked out the window at Cleveland unfolding before us and said: "Hmmm, looks like two Newarks."

■ ■ ■

By 1980, word had gotten around the world of politics that when Don Farmer of ABC News covered your candidacy, you

Chris and Don interview Bob Dole at the 1984 Republican Convention.

were doomed. Nevertheless, there I was, one viciously cold, snowy night in New Hampshire in January of 1980. I was there to cover the embryonic presidential campaign of Senator Bob Dole of Kansas. It was a campaign that remained embryonic.

He was holed up in a small, smoke-smelly room in the hotel in Manchester that politicians and press always stayed in. Apparently all the nicer, deodorized rooms had been taken by the 432 other Republicans who wanted to run against President Jimmy Carter that year.

I got there after dark, which in a New Hampshire winter means sometime after 3:00 p.m. Dole was gracious enough to invite me in for a chat. Did I say gracious? His first words to me were: "Don Farmer. Oh great, I see the network expects my campaign to take off any minute now."

That broke the ice. I didn't have the heart to tell him that it was my final assignment for ABC News; I was leaving in a month to join CNN in Atlanta. I just said that he was lucky he wasn't named George.

A FEW

FAVORITES

My old friend Frank Hyland used to cover the Hawks for the *Atlanta Journal*, and George Cunningham did the same for the morning paper, the *Constitution*. Both papers were owned by Cox Publishing, but nonetheless there was spirited competition between the two. The suits didn't care which paper got a story because all the money went into the same pockets, but the reporters and editors played it as if they were in a battle to the death with one another.

The executive sports editor of the *Journal* at the time was a tough and talented newsman named Jim Minter. We were on a West Coast roadtrip when Minter called Hyland and blistered him. It seems that Cunningham had come up with a couple of big stories ahead of Hyland. A dispirited Hyland, J&B Scotch bottle in hand, reported to my room one afternoon in San Francisco be-moaning his fate. A gin rummy game ensued and the Scotch bottle's contents dwindled dramatically. Hyland kept bitching about how unfair it all was.

What did I do? I tried to help, of course. "Look Frank," I said, "I'm employed by the Hawks, so you can call me an informed NBA source and you'll be technically at least half right. Quote this source as saying . . . oh, what the hell, Spencer Heywood is think-ing about jumping from the ABA to the NBA. He's going to sign with . . . oh, Seattle."

Hyland wrote the story — got some headlines — and felt the pressure was off him. Two weeks later he called me in shock. I'll be darned if Spencer Heywood hadn't jumped from the ABA to Seattle. I had no idea it was going to happen. Hyland became a hero, and his secret has always been safe with me — till now.

■ ■ ■

You know Dale Murphy won the Most Valuable Player award a couple of times, and you know he had a nice-guy image with the press and with the fans. The real story on Dale Murphy? He's an even better person than any of us have ever been able to explain. Dale is a Mormon — a member of the Church of the Lat-ter Day Saints. He was converted to Mormonism by his friend and former teammate Barry Bonnell. As devout as Murphy was in his beliefs, he never tried to talk you into seeing things his way.

Baseball humor is often very crude and very vulgar. Murph might wince when the four-letter words were flying; he might walk away . . . but you never heard him complain about it. Murphy would delight in buying dinner for his teammates, but they had to pay for their own alcoholic beverages. In short, Dale Murphy is the kind of young man that old men hope their kids will turn out to be. It would be impossible to be a nicer guy. He isn't little goody two-shoes. He's just a good man — one of the few people I have met in my life that cause you to try to be a little better yourself when you're around them.

There was a day in San Diego, though, when people saw that Murphy isn't just a milquetoast nice guy. A fan was deep into his cups and really giving it to the Braves from behind their dugout each time the team came in from the field. His language was horrible for about six innings, and it kept getting worse and worse. Murphy came trotting in from centerfield. He stopped in front of the dugout, eyes blazing, and said to the guy, "You will stop that kind of language and you will stop it now. You are embarrassing

Two-time National League Player of the Year (and all-time favorite Brave) Dale Murphy. (Courtesy Turner Broadcasting System)

yourself and the people around you." His teammates were shocked. The fan not only shut up. He got up and left the ballpark.

And Murphy was a gamer, too. One night he cut his hand badly as he made a great defensive play in the outfield. He couldn't play the next night because of the stitches and the swelling, but he did step in and slam a pinch-hit home run to win the game. Everybody was amazed that he could even stand the pain of swinging the bat, to say nothing of hitting one out of the ballpark.

Through the bad years the Atlanta Braves *were* Dale Murphy. He was about all the fans had to root for and identify with. He's a helluva (sorry about that, Murph) man, and I feel extremely fortunate to have had a chance to know him. It's so sad that he didn't get to share in the good years with this team. But you'll never hear him complain. He's a truly remarkable man.

■   ■   ■

Another of my favorite baseball characters was the late Rube Walker. Rube was a catcher for the Dodgers and the Cubs in his playing days and went on to become one of baseball's most successful pitching coaches. He helped develop the first batch of great hurlers for the Mets — guys like Tom Seaver, Jerry Koosman, Nolan Ryan and John Matlack. He later teamed with Bob Gibson as a co-pitching coach for the Braves during the Joe Torre years.

Rube was never a great player — but he was a good one. His only claim to infamy was that he was behind the plate and called the pitch that Bobby Thomson hit for a home run to win the pennant for the Giants over the Dodgers in 1951. It was the now famous "shot heard 'round the world" off Ralph Branca. It was the one thing Rube didn't want to talk about, so naturally it was *always* the focal point of conversation whenever Rube was within hearing distance.

One night, in fact, the Braves were flying out of Atlanta after a home game, headed for Pittsburgh and the start of another roadtrip. Thanks to the efforts of a somewhat obese broadcaster, aided and abetted by a somewhat bald one, it was arranged for the famous Russ Hodges call of the Thomson homer to be played on the airplane's P.A. system right after the stewardess and the captain got through with their on-air business. Rube heard it, reddened, and refused to turn around to confront those he knew were responsible, while the rest of the airplane dissolved in laughter.

On another occasion Rube was being interviewed by a young radio reporter on the bench in the Atlanta dugout. The kid was obviously just starting out. His questions were totally inane but Rube Walker was a nice man, a patient man, and he put up with all of this for about ten minutes while players and broadcasters tried very hard not to laugh in the kid's face. It looked like the thing was finally winding down when the kid said, "Mr. Walker, before I let you go, I have just one more question. What was the pitch Bobby Thomson hit to win the 1951 pennant for the Giants?" To which Rube replied, "He hit a bleeping home run." End of interview.

Rube was one of the most delightful men I have ever met and for all of us who knew him, his passing was a devastating loss.

■   ■   ■

Another unforgettable character who is no longer with us is Don Drysdale. A Hall of Fame pitcher and a terrific broadcaster, Don died of a heart attack in a Montreal hotel room in 1993.

What always impressed me about Drysdale was his humility. You never heard the word "I" from Don. He was as down to earth as they come. He was a friend to me, but was much closer to his former teammate and current Braves announcer Don Sutton. Don and I were working together on the night that news of his death flashed across the wire. Our stage manager handed the bulletin to Sutton, not realizing how close those two great righthanders had been. Don handed it to me with his hand shaking as if he had palsy. We just stared at one another in shock for what seemed like an eternity. Finally I hit both our "cough" switches and said something like, "Don, get the hell out of here." He did, and I continued with one of the worst broadcasts of my life.

The terrible news made it a thoroughly rotten night at the ballpark for every announcer who had the privilege of knowing Don Drysdale.

■   ■   ■

We had a pitcher back in the bad years by the name of Dave Campbell. His nickname was Chopper. He was a heckuva kid and a true blithe spirit. I remember his first roadtrip to New York when he hopped on the team bus all fired up about a stereo deal he had purchased out on the street. He raved about what a great deal he had gotten on his brand-name box. It broke, of course, after only a couple of days.

Chopper would also crack me up after a bad pitching outing when the long ball had hurt him. "Those goldarn fly-ball home runs are killing me," he would say. Many of those fly balls traveled more than 400 feet, but to Chopper they were fly-ball home runs and that was that.

THE ALWAYS COLORFUL CONGRESS

The Congress was never lackluster. Covering Capitol Hill always was more interesting than the White House beat. If the President is dull or boring, he's still President, and the office commands some respect. But in the Congress you have 535 men and women to cover, and there always are some great wackos among them.

One of the legendary members was Republican senator William L. Scott of Virginia. He served three terms in the House, one in the Senate, and left unforgettable moments in both. When he retired from the Senate, he said that his major achievement was engineering passage of a bill to set up a new holiday called "American Business Day." It failed in the House and disappeared.

Observers on the Hill, including those of us who covered the place, thought that Scott's greatest hit was when *New Times* magazine named him the "dumbest Congressman."

Keep in mind, *New Times* magazine was small, with limited circulation, so relatively few people saw the article about Scott's "award." But the senator called a news conference to deny that he was the dumbest guy in the Congress. Needless to say, the press conference guaranteed that the charge and his denial got major national coverage.

Even earlier, before I got the Congressional beat in 1975, Scott was named the "least bright" congressman in a poll by Ralph Nader's Capitol Hill News Service. Through the years, Scott's own antics reinforced the impression. The now-defunct *Washington Star* chronicled some of them, thanks to writer John Tierney.

■ In 1975 on a trip to the Middle East, Senator Scott said he was reluctant to go into a Moslem mosque because it wasn't "a Christian building."

■ After a senator compared his colleagues' refusal to act promptly to someone going through menopause, Scott was quoted as responding, "Well, it's a good thing it only comes once a month."

■ After his second junket to the Panama Canal, he was asked what he had learned from yet another trip at the taxpayers' expense. Senator Scott was quoted as saying: "The Canal Zone is ten miles wide, five miles on either side of the Canal." He also told reporters that he had seen ships going in two directions.

The *Washington Star* reported that Senator Scott had made forty trips to foreign countries, visiting many countries twice, during his six years in the Senate.

When he returned from that well-publicized visit to the Middle East, according to the *Star*, Scott reported to the Senate Armed Services Committee. He told the committee that the tour led him to conclude that Israel needed "a feeling of security . . . with the bordering nations," and that the Palestine Liberation Organization "seemed to pose a problem to Israel."

TWO OF THE MEN I MOST enjoyed covering were Senator Howard Baker of Tennessee and Senator Barry Goldwater of Arizona.

Senator Baker was forever a gentlemen, speaking ill of hardly anyone, particularly other Republicans, at least in public.

Senator Goldwater, however, was a man who always said what he meant when he meant it. About his colleague Senator Scott, Goldwater once said, "If he were any dumber, he'd be a tree."

■ ■ ■

One of the most bizarre men I ever met was the late Congressman Daniel Flood of Pennsylvania. He was a flamboyant former Shakespearean actor. In his seventies when I knew him, he often would appear on the floor of the House in suits that seemed to glow in the dark. He had been known to adorn himself with top hat, black cape, and Fred Astaire-type dancing cane.

One day radio reporter Gene Gibbons, who now is a White House correspondent, was doing a taped interview with Flood for UPI Audio.

Gene said, "Mr. Flood, this interview is for use on the air tomorrow. Tell me sir, how will your committee vote on the appropriations bill?"

"Well, young man," answered Flood, "I'll be able to tell you more after I consult with committee members at four o'clock this afternoon."

Gibbons stopped his tape and said, "Congressman, you see, this is for use tomorrow morning, so please don't refer to your meeting this afternoon. See, it'll be over when the interview airs."

"Oh, of course," said Flood.

Gene turned the tape on and asked, again, "How will your committee vote?"

Flood answered, "I'm not sure, but I'll have a better idea after I confer with the members at four o'clock this afternoon."

Exasperated, Gene hit the stop button again.

"Look, Mr. Flood, as I said, this is not for use now. It's on tape, for tomorrow, the morning news show. Your committee meeting is this afternoon, so by tomorrow that would already have been yesterday. Please, keep that in mind, OK?"

"Of course," said the congressman. "I understand perfectly now. Proceed."

Gibbons turned the tape on and asked, again, "Congressman, how will your committee vote on the appropriations bill?"

Said Mr. Flood, with authority and vigor: "Well, young man, I'll know a lot more about that, when I confer with my colleagues, at four o'clock yesterday afternoon."

COACHES

AND

MANAGERS

WHO'VE

CALLED

ATLANTA

HOME

I've been around a long time and have been fortunate enough to work with some interesting managers and coaches along the way. I thought I'd share a few thoughts about them.

■ Richie Guerin: Richie was the first pro coach I ever worked with, and he was a huge help to me. Richie was a man's man. He had been a tough Marine and a tough NBA player back in the days when no quarter was asked and none was given. A complex, emotional, extremely intelligent man, he went out of his way to make things easy for a young broadcaster. He also has become a huge success in the financial circles of his native New York.

■ Lenny Wilkens: Lenny was the Hawks' captain when I got the job. He and Richie didn't always agree about things, but Lenny was extremely forthcoming and helpful to me, and I think Lenny encouraged the other veterans of that very good Hawks team to be likewise. He should have been with the Hawks when they moved to the South in the late '60s. I was thrilled when he finally got to coach the team in 1993. His brilliant success has come as no surprise to me.

■ Cotton Fitzsimmons: A man who, Pete Maravich once said, was the only NBA coach small enough to sleep in a pillowcase. Fellow Missourians, Cotton and I hit it off from the start. He coached the Hawks in my days of running the streets between marriages, and he always brought me home to his house for Christmas dinner when my kids were 600 miles away, living in St. Louis. His kindness down through the years will never be forgotten, and his success in several NBA ports of call has been impressive.

■ Hubie Brown: One of the most intense people I have ever met. Hubie Brown saved the franchise in Atlanta but was unable to save himself careerwise. If a person can care too much about his job, then

Hubie Brown is guilty. His passion for his job was incredible, and he brings that same intensity to his work as a television commentator. He is always meticulously prepared. He's also a damn good friend and, away from the game, possesses a great sense of humor.

■ Kevin Loughery: A former player, an engaging Irishman, an extremely funny fellow. I always thought Kevin tried too hard to be the players' friend when he coached the Hawks. It got to the point where the players were doing the impossible. They were missing Hubie! It didn't work out for him in Atlanta, but he's doing well now as coach of the Miami Heat.

Former Hawks coach (and current Miami Heat coach) Kevin Loughery.
(Courtesy Turner Broadcasting System)

■ Mike Fratello: A protege of Hubie, but a good deal more than that. Michael is always prepared and at times can be very abrasive to his players. He's a street fighter, and I mean that as a compliment. He grew up on the streets of south Philly — the little guy who always had to fight for whatever he got. With Mike Fratello you always know where you stand. There should be more people who do business that way. Mike had a helluva year with a crippled team in Cleveland last year. He's as good a coach as there is, though, like Hubie, he doesn't suffer fools gladly. And fools abound in the NBA.

■ Dave Bristol: Dave was the first manager I worked with in Atlanta. I also hosted a weekly radio show he did on WRNG Radio — one of the first sports call-in shows in the South. We called it "Ask The Manager." How clever! That show was an unmitigated disaster. A caller would ask, "Dave, why don't you bat Darrell Evans fourth?" Dave would answer, "I'm the manager. I'll do what I want." Dave was a public relations nightmare because he always said what he thought. You can't do that anymore.

■ Joe Torre: Joe did everything backwards in Atlanta. In his first year he won a divisional title. In his second year he finished second. In his third year he finished tied for second and got fired. Had he done it the other way around, he would have gotten a lifetime contract. A delightful man, Torre had interests other than baseball, and that bothered some of the oldliners in the Braves' organization. They got him fired, and they often rued the day. His departure marked a downturn in the Braves' fortunes.

■ Eddie Haas: A career minor leaguer, Eddie was totally out of his element managing the big club. He's a nice man, but the players didn't like him and they didn't respect him. It was he on the award-winning "Eddie Haas Show" who once proudly responded to my question about who would be pitching for the Dodgers the next two days, "Venezuela and Horsehider." Enough said.

■ Chuck Tanner: Chuck has a lot of b-s about him, but he really got a bad rap in Atlanta. Some-body took down only a part of a quote of his, which began that he couldn't wait to ride down Peachtree Street in a parade after the Braves clinched a title. He went on to say that he knew it was going to be a difficult thing to do, but that he was confident that he could get it done. Unfortunate-ly, the only part of the quote anybody ever saw or remem-bered was the part about the parade. With the teams he had to manage, he was fortunate to not have a lynch mob chasing him in the other direction.

Former Hawks coach (and current Cleveland Cavalier coach) Mike Fratello.
(Courtesy Turner Broadcasting System)

■ Bobby Cox: A man with no ego, but with tremendous confidence in what he is doing. The consummate players' manager and one of the most patient men I have ever met. Bobby sincerely dislikes the spotlight. He likes to deflect the attention to others. Great guy.

YOU CAN'T TALK TO ME LIKE THAT, SIR!

For a journalist who's been in the field for a while, encountering the big names of the world becomes routine. Some of the biggies, though, prove to be less routine than others.

Take Helmut Schmidt, for example, the former chancellor of then West Germany. In my duties as the bureau chief for ABC News in Bonn, the West German capital, I had to interview the chancellor on occasion. The first time he made it clear how he felt about talking with some American TV type.

"What's your name, young man?" he asked at our first encounter.

"Don Farmer, sir," I replied.

"Farmer? Farmer?" he said, looking thoughtful.

"It would be 'Bauer' in German, Chancellor," I added brightly.

"Yes, of course. 'Peasant' is what it means. Well, how long will this take, Mr. Peasant?" he asked, eyebrows arched, eyes bulging.

From that point, it only *seemed* like a nine-hour interview.

Walter Mondale was a much nicer man. (Hell, "The Penguin," Batman's nemesis, was a nicer man than Helmut Schmidt.) I enjoyed covering Senator Mondale when he was Jimmy Carter's running mate in the presidential campaign of 1976.

Mondale and Carter took a few days off during the Republican convention that year. Carter went to Plains, Georgia. Mondale went to Hibbing, Minnesota. Actually he retreated to a nice lake house north of town, while the traveling press corps was billeted at a motel in Hibbing.

One day Mondale's senior advisor asked whether I'd like to play tennis with him and "the Senator." That would be Mondale, so I said sure; at least it would get me out of that Hibbing hotel for a couple of hours.

During the second set, Mondale and I were partners. I lunged for a serve, turned my ankle, and fell into a heap on the court.

"Come on, let's go," said Mondale, tapping his racket on the court.

I said it hurt like hell but that I would give it a try. When the ball came at me on the next volley, I reached for it, came down on the same ankle and collapsed.

"I gotta quit, Senator; this is a bad sprain," I told him.

He walked over to where I was sitting.

"Is there blood in your shoe?" he asked.

"Well, no, it's a sprain. No blood," I said.

"Then play tennis, now!" he responded and strode back to his position.

I was on crutches for two weeks. He was amused at that but still a bit irritated that his tennis partner had wimped out that day.

CELEBRITIES AND SUPERSTARS

I've had many thrills in the broadcasting business, but this is perhaps my greatest. I'm doing a Hawks game at the Forum in Los Angeles in the early '80s. Prior to the game I'm in the press room there, which is jammed not only with working press but with players' wives and celebrities as well.

I get tapped on the shoulder. I turn and a distinguished-looking gentleman somewhat diffidently says that he doesn't want to bother me, but that he's a big fan of mine from watching Braves games on cable and that he thinks I really know my stuff. For one of the few times in my life I can barely mutter a thank-you. That distinguished gentleman was Joe DiMaggio, who, as you know, is one of the greatest baseball players of all time. I floated through that NBA game. When you've got Joe DiMaggio going for you, you're in pretty tall cotton.

That's one of the nice things about my job. I get to meet a lot of interesting people — movie stars and various other celebrities. For instance, John Goodman has told me that he listened to me broadcast University of Missouri football games when he was a kid. I got to grow up knowing Stan Musial, another truly great ballplayer and person. I worked with the great Henry Aaron on a few games when he filled in as an analyst on some Braves games. For such a quiet man he did a helluva job on the air.

I've got a theory about superstars. I think most of them are really nice people. I also think it's harder and harder for superstars to act like nice people because of the constant pressure placed upon them by the seemingly endless parade of radio/television/tabloid/ newspaper types. I've been in press conferences where I was honestly embarrassed by the stupidity of the questions we ask these people. It is no wonder that some of them are distrustful of the press. Many in our business earn that distrust and make it harder on the decent, honest journalists who are just out to do a job.

I'll never forget the night Pete Rose's long National League hitting streak was stopped in Atlanta by the tandem of Larry McWilliams and Gene Garber. The first question asked of Rose in the news conference was, "Are you glad it's over?" If Pete had wanted it to be over he would have gone in the tank a long time ago. It really can get ridiculous.

CELEBRI-TUDE

Chris and I interviewed a lot of celebrities on that now-defunct "Take Two" program on CNN. We didn't always learn a lot from the on-air interviews, but we got some valuable lessons in real life from their off-air antics. The abuse that some celebrities spread around often lands on people who work behind-the-scenes in TV.

The kind, patient woman who was our

researcher was having lunch at her desk at CNN Atlanta one day, a salad of some sort, when singer Larry Gatlin walked in. He was scheduled for a live "Take Two" interview in about thirty minutes.

"Boy, that looks good," he said to the researcher, eyeballing her lunch. Gatlin then plunged his open hand into the salad, pulled out a fistful, and ate it.

The woman was astounded, but Larry Gatlin acted as though he does that sort of thing every day. Maybe he does.

■ ■ ■

Staffers on the "Take Two" show will never forget Lily Tomlin, her female traveling companion, and their dog.

Tomlin swept into the CNN studios for a live interview in a bear of a bad mood. Her companion carried the Tomlin dog, a small, nasty thing, which through no fault of its own, apparently had developed the personality of its owner.

The other woman plopped the dog on the desk of the woman who books guests for interviews and said, "Have somebody feed and walk the dog."

No "please," no "thank you," just a barking of orders from an unpleasant woman accustomed to being obeyed.

While she and the dog intruded on the staff, Lily Tomlin was busy making enemies in her own way. First, she borrowed our researcher's hairbrush and makeup and used them. Then she looked at the interview set and complained about the lighting. As the eager young CNN staffers whirled around her, working on the lights, she continued to complain.

We tried small talk to distract her, but she was obsessed with the lighting. Then she said she might have to leave.

"I can't do this; it's not right," she repeated, standing up as if to walk out, then sitting down, up, down, up down.

In the end, she stayed for the interview and was charming, while doing her many wonderful characters. On air, she was her talented self. Off air, the guest from hell. We liked her dog better; at least he couldn't help being the way he was.

■ ■ ■

Harlan Ellison, the science fiction writer who had branched out into other literary endeavors, was scheduled for a live satellite interview from New York.

I had written a short introduction to the interview, explaining to the audience that Ellison was one of the premier science fiction writers of our day. What I didn't know was, Ellison did not like to be called a science fiction writer. It was as though Reggie Jackson didn't want to be called a great baseball player ever again, but insisted on the term "super athlete."

So as we read the intro on camera, live, Ellison heard the term "science fiction writer," got up from his chair, and walked off the set. When the director switched from us on camera from Atlanta to the New York studio, all we had to interview was an empty chair. We made the appropriate apologies, not really sure at that point why Ellison had left, and went to a commercial.

But I recall with some satisfaction that we used the term "science fiction writer" one more time in our explanation of our missing guest. I hope he heard it as he was leaving the studio.

■ ■ ■

Some celebrities are so self-absorbed that they don't even seem to realize their behavior bothers other people.

Sylvester Stallone came in for a live interview one day, and Sasha, his wife at the time, was with him. Stallone was fine but his

Chris and Don interview First Lady Nancy Reagan on CNN's "Take Two" program.

wife was a pill. She sat at a desk normally used for work by our guest booker. Doing their best to be polite, the staffers tried to strike up a conversation.

All of a sudden, Sasha Stallone propped her feet up on the booker's desk, took off her shoes and began painting her toenails. She never mentioned it and apparently didn't think anything of it. Maybe in her circles, people often lapse into fits of toenail grooming during office conversations with strangers.

■ ■ ■

On the air, the two worst interviews we ever did on "Take Two" were with Harrison Ford and Lee Marvin.

Ford had just completed *Raiders of the Lost Ark*; it was a smash, and he was just about to become a big star. But not if he had to ad-lib. We asked him about the movie, knowing never to ask questions that can be answered with a "yes" or a "no." But he found ways to use those answers anyway. We switched to his personal life, focusing on his reputation as an accomplished carpenter. Again, we got nothing but nods, grimaces, and three-word answers.

He's probably much better at it these days. Maybe we are too.

Lee Marvin was hopeless. To most of our questions, he grunted. It was 9:00 a.m. in Los Angeles when we did the interview, and maybe that explained it. For him, "yes" was an essay and "no" was a monologue.

When you ask a celebrity, "How are you feeling?" and the answer comes back, "Yes," you know that it's time to move on. We did, and he seemed relieved and happy about it.

■ ■ ■

Then there are the good guys, the wonderful celebrities who got to the top with talent and took their good sense and courtesy with them on the way to stardom.

Dudley Moore is one of them. He was on live to promote his film *Arthur*, but he was willing to talk about anything, with charm and grace. He charmed our staff and was as nice off-air as on.

Robert Duvall was another gem. He had just finished a movie about gypsies and seemed to know as much about the subject as he did about himself. He was also fascinated with CNN. He came early, enjoyed looking around the studios, and was reluctant to leave after the on-air interview.

Bob Hope also was gracious and entertaining, as pleasant and professional off the air as on. It must be hard for people like him to stay humble, since people are so in awe when he arrives. All eyes are on him, from the studio to the men's room.

And that reminds me of Alan Alda. The men's room, I mean.

Shortly after he arrived at the CNN headquarters for an interview, Alda asked where the men's room was located. Our booker told him, and Alda asked her to accompany him. She did, and when they reached the door of the rest room, Alda asked the woman to please "stand guard" outside the door until he came out. She did that, too.

Afterward, Alda explained.

"When you're a well-known actor, scriptwriters, producers, and other would-be's have a trick of catching you in the men's room," he said. "You're a captive audience, and they make their pitch before you can zip up and get out."

Alda then told our booker a story about Burt Lancaster, who was standing at a urinal in a men's room in a hotel somewhere. A mirror lined the wall above the fixtures. Another man walked up to the urinal next to Lancaster, looked up into the mirror, and suddenly realized who was standing next to him.

"Oh my God, it's Burt Lancaster," the man said, turning to face Lancaster and spraying the superstar as he turned.

LIFE *in* THE EMPIRE

THE

BIG T

Naturally I have to give you my views of my charismatic boss, Ted Turner. If I detested him I'd have to lie about it, but I hope you will believe me when I say he is one of the most fascinating men I have ever met in my life. Let me give you some examples of Turner, up close and personal, that might help you understand what kind of guy he is:

ONCE WHEN TED traveled to St. Louis with us, we decided to go to dinner together after the game. Pete, Ernie, Ted, and I were driving my brother Chris's car, and soon after we left the stadium, the car developed a flat. I wheeled it into a grimy gas station downtown and asked the man how much he would charge to change the tire. He said five dollars, but Turner piped up that he would change it for three. We moved off the gas station's lot, and he changed it in record time, collecting a dollar from each of us. He is, without question, the most down-to-earth rich person I have ever met in my life.

■ ■ ■

Under Turner's stewardship of the Hawks and Braves there have been some good times, but, brother, there have been some bad years as well. Here I am, under Turner's employ, going on the air each night and announcing how lousy his teams are. Never once in all those years did he ask me to lay off. Never did he bitch about my being negative or try to force me to be more positive about his clubs. Most announcers don't get the kind of leeway Ted Turner has offered me, and his willingness to let us do it our way has made my job much easier. It has also, I think, made me a better broadcaster.

■ ■ ■

The only two things Turner has gotten angry at me about were 1) making fun of his movies and 2) telling him how much to pay me. The movie thing was simple. As you are broadcasting a game, somebody hands you a promotion card to read. It announces what the next program is — in those days almost always a movie, and almost always a bummer. It seemed that every other night *The*

Creature From the Black Lagoon was the postgame entertainment. I couldn't help it. Those movies made me laugh, and he would go crazy. His fit would last ten minutes or so, and all would be well again.

THE TIME HE FIRED ME WAS an even better story. It was time to negotiate my contract again. I had done the preliminary work with Bob Wussler, the former CBS-TV president who was Turner's number-one aide. Wussler said that Ted would come in at, say, $40,000. I should say $60,000, at which Ted would bitch and moan and finally offer $45,000. Then, said Wussler, you say $50,000, and you can settle for $48,000. That was agreeable to me.

The deal went just as it was supposed to for awhile — up until we got to his offer of $45,000, just as Wussler had predicted. I countered with 50K, just like Wussler said I should. Turner stayed at $45,000. Now I felt sure that Wussler had steered me straight, so I finally said, "Look, Ted, let's quit bleeping around. I'm yours for $48,000." He stayed at $45,000. I said, "Is this your final offer?" He said yes.

I *knew* he was bluffing as I headed toward the door . . . until I heard him say, "You dumb s.o.b., how can you leave all this?" I kept walking. The door slammed behind me and I walked five feet down the hall, past Wussler's secretary and into his office where he was holding a big meeting. I said, "Nice going pal, you just got me fired." Wussler is a beauty. He gave me great advice. He told me to go home and say nothing to anyone. That's exactly what I did.

Thank God Paula was working. There was nobody home. Each time the phone rang, I leaped to it praying it was Wussler. About the third time it rang, it turned out to be Ernie. I wasn't supposed to work that night because it was a non-televised game, but Pete had become ill and Ernie asked me if I would pinch hit. I couldn't help it, I started laughing. I said, "Ernie, I'd love to help, but if I show up to work, *you* might get fired." I suggested he call Wussler. Wussler called me and told me to go to the ballpark, do the game, and keep quiet. I did.

Ted approached before the game started. "Let's not let it end like this . . . $47,500," he offered. To this day I believe he just wanted to show Wussler he could get me a little cheaper than Wussler thought he could. It was a scary day but a perfect example of the pre-CNN Turner in action.

■ ■ ■

If people only knew how much Ted did for the city of Atlanta, they would be amazed. It was only his determination that got the Olympic Stadium under construction. Some people talked about the Braves taking advantage of the city and of the Olympic people here in town, but, believe me, Ted Turner could have gotten a much better deal in at least two other municipalities in the Atlanta area. It is his sincere belief that without a vibrant downtown area Atlanta becomes a second-class city, and that's why he hung tough to help get this stadium underway. He is truly one of the most remarkable men and unforgettable characters I've ever met. And he's also made me a reasonably wealthy man, for which, come to think of it, I now thank him.

To sum up Ted Turner, I can only say that he was my friend before I ever worked for him and I hope that he still is. After twenty-plus years, that's (as he would say) "not too shabby."

PRESIDENT

TED

TURNER?

I think the only time Ted Turner ever got mad at me was when I quit CNN.

I was very tired of just reading the news at CNN, tired of dealing with the office politics at the middle management level, and eager to try something new — local TV news in Atlanta. Ted didn't think that was very smart. He probably was right.

I was leaving on a matter of principle, after a long and anguish-filled series of disputes with a middle manager at CNN. It had nothing to do with my respect and admiration for Ted, which I have to this day. But he seemed to see it as a question of my loyalty to him. That wasn't it at all, but our friendship deteriorated after that, and I always will regret it.

Working for Ted Turner in the early days of CNN was a mixture

Chris and Don interviewing their boss at a 1983 cable industry convention.

of the sublime and the absurd. The following incident was both.

Chris and I attended the Goodwill Games in Moscow in 1986 and spent a lot of time with Ted and Janie Turner, his wife at the time. One afternoon Ted and I sat in the mostly empty stands at the stadium where a casual rehearsal was underway for the opening ceremonies the following night.

We were just chatting about nothing much, watching the athletes, when Ted, still looking out at the field, abruptly asked, "What would it take to run for President?"

I looked at him and knew better than to ask the direct question whether he meant *him* running for President.

"Well, you have enough money, and you could raise enough for sure, but are you sure you want to go through that?"

"No, no, not at all. I just wondered what a guy would have to do, where to start, when to do it and all that sort of thing." He added that he probably wouldn't even consider it, but was just making conversation.

I knew the idea had occurred to him before, but he clearly had not yet pondered the enormity of the task. I explained that I had covered a lot of presidential candidates, none of whom had ever won, and that I would be happy to put some thoughts on paper for him.

He said that would be great and changed the subject.

A month or so later I gave him a lengthy report on building an organization, dealing with the party of his choice (I was never sure which party he might choose to represent), and all the thousands of things one would have to do to run a serious campaign for a major party presidential nomination. I wrote about primaries and fundraising and campaign advertising. I wrote about the inevitable probing into a candidate's personal life.

Ted thanked me for the report, and that's the last I ever heard of it or of his reaction to it. As I write, he has not run for President, but don't forget — he owns the rights to *that* movie and its famous closing line, "Tomorrow is another day."

THE BRAVES' FRONT OFFICE

Covering the Atlanta Braves the past four seasons has been like a dream come true. You can't ask for more than highly competitive teams and crowds of better than 40,000 every time the team plays at home.

Three people deserve the credit. First, there's Ted Turner, who shelled out the bucks in the first place. Following him are General Manager John Schuerholz and Manager Bobby Cox. Their ability to work together has been the key ingredient of the Braves' wonderful run. And when you stop to think about it, both of those men deserve a great deal of credit for their ability to sublimate their own egos and work for the common good.

Consider the situation. Bobby Cox has to fire Russ Nixon as manager and step down from the front office and become the manager again. He is replaced in the general manager's office by Schuerholz, who had completed a successful run as general manager in Kansas City. It would have been perfectly understandable for Schuerholz to have fired Cox and brought in his own man to run the Braves down on the field. It would have stamped the Braves as his team, and it would have also removed from the scene the man who had occupied his chair in the previous regime.

On the other side of the coin there was Cox — one of the game's most respected managers — who could have let his ego get in the way and gone elsewhere. But Bobby loved Atlanta, and Schuerholz had always admired the way Cox managed the Blue Jays when they competed against the Royals. Thus the deal was done, and what a partnership it has been. The Braves were a disaster on the field when Bobby was in the front office, but it was he who made the trade to bring John Smoltz to the organization, and it was under his stewardship that David Justice, Ron Gant, Steve Avery, Tom Glavine, Jeff Blauser, and others were developed. And then it was Schuerholz who brought Terry Pendleton, Rafael Belliard, Sid Bream, Alejandro Pena, Otis Nixon, and Deion Sanders into the fold. Their ability to work together has been a huge part of the success enjoyed by the Atlanta team. And as you gaze on down the road, the Braves look to be contenders not just in '94 and '95, but on into the foreseeable future.

I get a kick out of remembering my first real conversation with Schuerholz. He and I had a mutual friend who lived in Kansas City at the time — a top-flight television director named Lonnie Dale who suggested to John that he talk to me as soon as he got to town to get an overview of the team from someone who was fairly close to the situation but not on the payroll of the ballclub. I picked him up at the ballpark one day, and we headed to Bone's Restaurant in fashionable Buckhead to dine. After the usual pleasantries Schuerholz said, "Okay, tell me what you think I should know about the Atlanta Braves."

I talked for about thirty-five minutes nonstop. By the time I had finished talking John had finished his lunch. What I had to say had not been pleasant, but I had been as honest as I could possibly be. I then told him, "John, I checked the airline guide before we came over here. We can do one of two things. I can take you back to the ballpark, or there's a 2:20 flight nonstop back to Kansas City. Take your pick." Thank God he decided to stick it out. He is one of the sharpest executives I have ever seen in action — totally prepared at all times and normally one step ahead of the opposition.

Speaking of executives, I think I should say a word about Stan Kasten, a man who wears two hats as president of both the Hawks and the Braves. Stan's is an interesting story. He's a guy who could have been a helluva lawyer; he was good enough to graduate with honors from the prestigious Columbia School of Law. But Stan was also a guy with an abiding passion for professional sports — so abiding, in fact, that when he came to work for Ted Turner, his initial salary was absolutely nothing. I kid him to this day that that was the only time he was compensated fairly.

In any event, he soon proved his worth and has worked his way into a very, very big job. He's the guy who brought Schuerholz to Atlanta. And he's the guy who brought Pete Babcock and Lenny Wilkens in to turn the Hawks into winners again. Have all his decisions been right? Of course not; nobody bats a thousand. But, on balance, you'd have to give the guy a very high grade. I'm only grateful that I don't have to negotiate with him. They say he is one of the shrewdest and savviest guys around when it comes to doing deals with people in the world of athletics. I know he's been a positive influence on the Turner empire.

That brings us to the subject of agents, the most vilified people in all of sports. There is some justification for that vilification. We all know the stories of agents who have robbed their young and unsuspecting clients. We have all read about the slimeballs who sign kids up before their college eligibility is over, thereby putting the kid and the school at risk. Yes, there are agents like that; but there are also agents who care about their clients, who are honorable and decent men, and who are really good at their jobs. Of course, those are the agents you never read about or hear about.

There is one thing about agents I don't understand. An agent takes a percentage of the gross whenever they do a deal for you. But here's where they lose me. Say a player is offered $300,000 a year going in. The agent finally makes the deal for $500,000. Why should he get a percentage of the first $300,000? The player could have gotten that much without the agent. Someday the players are going to figure that out, I think.

LIVE

FROM

HAVANA

So how's your trip to Cuba coming?" It was Ted Turner asking. He had stopped by our little office at CNN one day in late March of 1982, curious about what we would be putting on his network in our upcoming broadcasts from Havana.

We were going to Cuba to do a week of live programs in large part because Ted had recently returned from a personal visit with Fidel Castro.

He enjoyed his time with the Cuban dictator, fishing, hunting, swapping stories, smoking very good cigars.

We outlined our plans for our show, "Take Two." It would be the first time an American network would broadcast programs live from Havana since the revolution there.

Ted asked the cost and we told him — $100,000.

"Oh my God," he said as he threw up his hands. "We're spending a hundred grand or more to send you on a two-week vacation to Cuba."

Our visit to Cuba, in early April, was very different from Ted's, but he was the inspiration for it and supported it against those critics who thought it was giving Castro a propaganda freebie.

Ted also got some stuffed ducks out of the deal.

One night, late, near the end of our visit, the Cuban official assigned to us, Benvenido Abierno, knocked on the hotel room door of CNN producer and guest booker Gail Evans.

"I have a very important gift for you to take to Ted Turner," he said. "It's from Fidel!"

He handed Gail a large wooden box. In it were forty-eight Cuban cigars.

He then gave her a three-foot-long board, on which were mounted three scrawny stuffed ducks.

"What's with the ducks?" Gail asked.

Sr. Abierno explained that Ted had shot them while he and Fidel were hunting in Cuba several weeks earlier.

"Fidel had them stuffed and mounted and wants you to take them to Mr. Turner," he said.

Gail explained that we never would be able to get the stuff through U.S. Customs. The long-standing and still-existent U.S. economic embargo on Cuba made it illegal to trade with that country.

"The cigars are illegal in the U.S.," she told him. "And any customs official probably will cut open the ducks, looking for drugs."

But the Cuban was insistent, so Gail took the cigars and the ducks and we brought them back with us to Miami.

We were on a chartered flight, so our customs clearance was at a small shed, away from the main terminal. Gail asked to speak to the head customs official, who frowned a lot when she showed him the cigars and the ducks.

"They're for Ted Turner, a gift from Fidel Castro," she said.

"Are they big buddies?" asked the customs guy, skeptical.

"Well, Mr. Turner was in Cuba on a private visit, and Mr. Castro wanted him to have the ducks he shot and the cigars he likes," Gail explained.

"And I know you'll want to check inside the ducks, but if you do, just keep 'em, because they'll be worthless to my boss if they're mutilated," she continued.

The customs man said he wanted to confer with his colleagues. He went into a back room, then emerged a short time later with three other uniformed officials.

"Tell them what you told me," he said to Gail.

So she did — the Turner visit to Cuba, the hunting trip, the gifts, etc.

Silence. No reaction.

Then all four customs officials broke into laughter, shaking their heads.

"Tell Ted we like the Braves on TV, so we hope he enjoys the cigars and the ducks," the head man said as he waved Gail and her Cuban cargo out of the customs office.

■ ■ ■

Two CNN staffers, booker Gail Evans and director Guy Pepper, made a survey trip to Cuba in early March of 1982 before we took the "Take Two" show there for broadcast. When they returned to Atlanta, Gail and Guy urged the rest of us who were going — producer Katie Couric, associate producer Calvin Houts, correspondent Mike Boettcher and Chris and me — to take food with us. They said that food was scarce or bad or both in Cuban hotels and restaurants.

Gail and Guy also wanted to make at least a gesture toward observing Passover, which occurred while we were there. So they took several boxes of unleavened bread, matzoh, in their luggage when we all went to Havana on April 3.

Good thing they did, too.

The staple snack food in Cuba in 1982 was pork rinds. I'm not sure about breakfast, but I know they were served with lunch and dinner. They were greasy and salty and nasty, but we ate them.

We wondered why there was not plenty of fresh fish in Cuba, being an island nation. Our guide explained to us that many Cubans, at least in 1982, thought of fish as "peasant" food, consumed only by people who could not afford meat.

It seemed that Cuba's most abundant source of cheap, healthy food was treated with disdain. We would have traded all the pork rinds in Havana for a broiled grouper, but it wasn't to be had. The menu in the restaurant of the Hotel Nacional, once a luxury resort, could have won a literary prize for fiction. After a couple of days, we learned to ignore it and just ask the waiter what was available.

What was available was chicken. It was cooked one way, the same way, every day — greasy, probably fried in the fat left over from the pork rinds.

So the crispy, clean matzoh became the staple for all of us. Especially when we discovered that the peanut butter we had taken along went pretty well with it.

On Passover, Gail and Guy took the matzoh, minus the peanut butter, to the hotel dining room. A prosperous-looking Cuban sitting nearby noticed and approached them. He leaned over to Gail and whispered, "Are you a member of the tribe?"

Gail was startled, but smiled and looked up at the man.

"What do you mean?" she asked, not getting his point.

"The tribe, the tribe," he repeated, still in a whisper, glancing at the matzoh on her plate.

It then dawned on Gail that he was asking whether she was Jewish. Turned out he was too. He also was an active member of the Communist Party and a product of Soviet schooling. He had been assigned by the Castro government to watch us. He was enthusiastic about meeting American Jews, and he offered Gail a tour of the Jewish community in Havana.

It was a strange Passover for Gail and Guy, shunning pork rinds, sharing their matzoh with us and the Communist Cuban Jew who wanted to make friends, at least for a couple of weeks.

■ ■ ■

Katie Couric was the spark plug of our precedent-setting programming. People who know her now as the wake-up star of the "Today" show would have seen the seeds of her star status in her work in Cuba.

Katie was the producer of our "Take Two" program when we took the show to Cuba, and she also did a lot of on-air reports for the show.

"To call it a skeleton crew would be to give it the best possible status," Katie said recently of our trip to Cuba. She had for comparison the "Today" show trip to Cuba a decade later, in 1992.

"That second time, we had lots of people, laying cable, doing our makeup, all the rest of it," Katie said. "But I remember more about our 'Take Two' days there for some reason."

That's probably because nine of us did it all, fifteen hours of live TV, the first such programming from Cuba since Castro took over.

My most vivid memories of Katie in Havana include her sprawled on the floor of the room in the Nacional Hotel, papers and notebooks strewn about, doing a format for the shows, wondering whether scheduled guests would show up. Katie, however, has a different number one memory:

"I was the only one of us who had a toilet seat in the bathroom," she reminded me. "I was singularly blessed, I guess."

And she was. The rest of us had toilets in our hotel bathrooms, but no toilet seats.

That was just one of the many shortages in Cuba at that time. Apparently, Castro's government had not been able to convince its Soviet pals to provide toilet seats, and the U.S. economic embargo prevented Cuba from getting toilet seats from America. Keep in mind, the toilets were American made, installed in the luxury hotels in the days when Cuba was a posh resort island, so maybe Soviet toilet seats would not fit anyway. Whatever the reason, Cuba was, for the most part, toilet-seat free.

Not having a seat on a cold, porcelain toilet can make a visitor to Cuba cranky on a regu-

One of the infamous seatless toilets at Havana's Nacional Hotel. (Chris Curle)

lar basis. Consequently, eight of the nine CNN people who did that historic TV show in Havana were cranky a lot. But not Katie, and for the longest time, we didn't know why.

When we checked into the Nacional, one of the best hotels in Cuba, the lack of toilet seats didn't seem so important. And the Cubans tried to minimize the problem by putting those little sanitary paper wraps around the toilet bowl itself. That helped a lot, of course.

After a few days, however, trying to navigate the commode without falling into it became a daily irritant. We figured out why Katie, alone, was always in such relatively good spirits when she finally admitted, with devilish delight, that she was the only one among us who had a seat on her john.

I sometimes think that it was a formative event in Katie's life. When you see her today, smiling and joking or serious and concerned, you can tell that she has a healthy, confident, positive outlook on life. When she can smile at Bryant Gumble and other potential nuisances of the nineties, it may well be because she never had to go two weeks without a toilet seat in Cuba, don't you think?

■　■　■

Like the typical producer on low-budget CNN programs, Katie got to handle a lot of less-than-glamorous chores — like, for instance, arranging food for the rest of the staff. In Cuba in the spring of 1982, that often meant getting the soggy box lunches that were the only things available from the hotel for takeout.

Every day, as we prepared for the program from El Morro Castle, Katie would show up with the box lunches, smiling through the groans of the rest of us. Actually she groaned more loudly than anyone.

"Those box lunches were disgusting," she told me recently, obviously retaining vivid memories of the pork rinds, the greasy chicken, and the hard bread. She went on to share some other recollections.

"Do you recall that dance the Cubans did then?" she asked. I didn't.

"It was called the Double Dust Bust and they did it all the time," she said. My mind was a blank.

"How about those old cars?" she said. Yes, we had all experi-

Don along with "Take Two" crew members Katie Couric and Mike Boettcher at Havana's El Bodeguita restaurant. (Chris Curle)

enced mental flashbacks to "Mayberry" or "Happy Days" while watching the traffic in Havana.

Most of the cars, then and now, were vintage American Chevys and Fords from the fifties. They were plentiful in the pre-Castro days, when Americans used Cuba as a no-rules, all-fun playground. But when Castro took over and the Americans pulled out, the cars of the fifties, those garish-finned emblems of our presence, stayed behind. And no new American cars have been brought into Cuba since. Many are still running, held together by Cuban ingenuity, coddled by the few people lucky enough to own them.

The Cubans with money or influence have had access to Soviet-made cars in the past thirty years, but most Cubans don't like them. They didn't much like the Russians who lived in Havana either. In unguarded moments, we heard Cubans referring to Russians they'd see on the street as *bolos*, which means bowling pins in Spanish.

On our fourth day in Cuba, our whole crew went to a restaurant in Havana called El Bodeguita del Medio — still famous because Ernest Hemingway used to hang out there. Hemingway is a national hero in Cuba and his haunts are major tourist attractions.

At El Bodeguita, we ate the mediocre food and drank the mojitas and let the Hemingway mystique wash over us. The walls of the place are covered with the names of tourists and others who have gone there to be where Hemingway used to spend a lot of time eating, drinking, and being Ernest.

Katie's name is on the wall there somewhere, along with the rest of the CNN crew. She was so impressed with the Hemingway stuff that she went to the small country town where he wrote *The Old Man and the Sea* and did a story on the author, the town, and the irony of Cubans having such hero worship for an American writer. It was a good report and we ran it on our "Take Two" show from Havana later in the week.

It had an immediate impact back at CNN headquarters in Atlanta. Earlier in the year, then-president of CNN Reese Schoenfeld had said that he didn't want Katie doing on-air reports. He thought she looked too young and didn't have enough credibility. So Katie was stunned as well as pleased when Reese phoned her in Cuba right after her report on Hemingway aired.

"He said it was brilliant," she told me.

■ ■ ■

An attractive, smart, dedicated Communist named Amaryllis was our official interpreter in Cuba. Her English was good, her knowledge of Cuban history was excellent, and her loyalty to Fidel Castro was complete. Amaryllis met her match, however, while trying to handle a bunch of TV people, Americans and Cubans who were excited about what they were doing and excitable even in relatively calm situations.

Her frustration with the linguistic challenge of TV came to a head one very hot day at El Morro Castle, in the Havana harbor.

El Morro was the location for our live broadcast of the "Take Two" show. Originally built by the Spanish in 1589, El Morro had been used as a prison until 1978, at which point it was transformed into a museum and tourist stop. It offered a lovely look at Havana, but the setting was not ideal for television. The wind blew constantly, and the horseflies were intolerable. A temporary wooden shed shielded us from the sun, but the directors and other technicians sweltered inside a small control truck.

The Cuban director spoke no English and our man, Guy Pepper, had no Spanish, so the interpreter, Amaryllis, stood between them, translating one to the other. But she had done presidents and sports stars and media people many times in her career, so the first few minutes of Monday morning, April 12, were not too bad there in the control truck. The directors were calm and businesslike, setting their shots, discussing audio, lighting, and whatnot. Amaryllis was cool, competent, in control.

Then we hit air, the show began, and the directors went into the frenzy that often occurs in a live TV show.

There was that pesky six-second delay in audio, caused by the roundabout satellite path we had to use. Because of the trade embargo against Cuba, we were not allowed to send our signal by satellite directly to Landover, Maryland, which then was the normal way to reach the U.S. by international satellite. So the temperature and the noise level in the control truck increased as Guy and his Cuban counterpart barked orders, getting the signal up to the

Soviet "Intersputnik" satellite.

It was down-linked in Prague, Czechoslovakia, then up again on Intelsat to London, down to another satellite, then to Landover, then to CNN headquarters in Atlanta.

That, plus the other obvious problems in a bilingual productions effort, made the directors even more frenetic.

At the end of the three-hour program, the first person out of the control truck was Amaryllis — shaking and perspiring heavily.

"I can't do that again. I just cannot do it," she cried.

We asked why. "They don't even need an interpreter," she said harshly, referring to Guy Pepper and the Cuban director.

"Why not?" asked Gail Evans.

"All they do is scream *fuck* and *shit*!" Amaryllis said. She walked away, shaking her head.

The international directors' language had prevailed.

THE BEST BROAD-CAST TEAM IN BASEBALL

Our varied backgrounds, I think, help explain why our broadcast team has enjoyed so much success these past few years. (I assume we're successful since we're still working.) In Pete and myself you have two non-jocks who do the majority of the play-by-play with vastly differing styles. In Don Sutton we have a future Hall of Famer (who should be in already) who amassed more than 300 career victories and was a superstar. In Joe Simpson we have a guy who was a solid major league talent, but who will tell you that virtually every year of his career he had to win his major league job in spring training. So, not only do we have a pitcher and a hitter — who would naturally look at things differently — but we also have two men who, because of their respective attainments, obviously look at the game differently. That difference is the spice that I think and hope makes our broadcasts special.

Skip's mentor Ernie Johnson, Sr.
(Courtesy Turner Broadcasting System)

I might as well talk about my partners while we're on the subject. I was so lucky as a kid to get to work with Jack Buck on college basketball games and in some studio situations. I think that, thanks to him, I've developed a better sense of humor about what it is we do. From my dad, of course, I got the enthusiasm and love of the game which was there long before I started broadcasting. Traveling with him to Ebbets Field, the Polo Grounds — all the old ballparks I can barely remember. But at least I got to see them.

Since I started with the Braves, I've always worked with Pete, and we were broken in by a man we both love and respect, Ernie Johnson, Sr. I'll never forget the first game I worked with Ernie. It was a Braves spring training game in, I think, Orlando. Ernie and I opened the TV broadcast, and Pete had the radio. I did the starting lineups and all the pregame stuff and then, voice blaring, I said, "Jerry Royster standing in for Atlanta . . . and here to bring you the play-by-play story, the voice of the Braves, Ernie Johnson." He thanked me and did the first half inning.

During the break he put his arm around my shoulder and said, "Skip, if you don't mind, we're all the voices of the Braves, okay?" Here was the number-one guy saying we were all on an equal footing. Ernie had worked as the "number-two man" behind Milo Hamilton for many years. Milo is an immensely talented announcer with an ego as large as his considerable talent. From him, Ernie had learned some things that were good to do and a few things that were good not to do. He's like a big brother to me. I love the man and his family and am particularly proud of Ernie Johnson, Jr., finally getting the recognition he deserves as the best studio sports host in the world.

Then there's Pete Van Wieren, dubbed "The Professor" by Ernie. Pete is a consummate professional. His serious delivery belies the fact that he has a great sense of humor. He is never at a loss for words, and whatever sport he tries he handles to perfection. He's low-key and serious while I'm up tempo and a little bit insane, so I think we complement each other very well. After a game we've been known to have "just one" together a time or two as well.

Then there's Curly. Don Sutton was a great pitcher, and he was a great pitcher without having great talent. I mean that as a compliment. Don utilized every single iota of what talent the good Lord did give him. As a result, he knows an awful lot about both the mental and the physical aspects of pitching and winning in the major leagues. If you had to criticize Don for anything it would be that he's too quick of a study. He can watch a pitcher he has never seen before, and by the end of the first inning he will have told you all you need to know about the guy. He's a terrific announcer, and we're very lucky to have him, but I swear he would be the greatest pitching coach who ever lived if that was what he wanted to do.

"The best broadcast team in baseball" — Joe Simpson, Skip Caray, Don Sutton, and Pete Van Wieren. (Courtesy Turner Broadcasting System)

Then there's Joe Simpson, a former Dodger and Mariner. Joe left the security of Seattle where he was extremely popular to sign a one-year deal with WTBS to broadcast Braves games. I'll never forget his first quote in the papers in Atlanta when he was asked about the lack of security that a one-year deal provided. Said Joe, "Look, I feel like I'm here for life." That gamble has paid off richly for him, for us, and especially for our listeners. A dry sense of humor, a great work ethic —Joe is just a really good guy. The four of us have an awful lot of fun together, and I think that shows on the air too. As

Former Braves announcer John Sterling is now with the New York Yankees. (Courtesy Turner Broadcasting System)

somebody once said, "It's a long summer and a small booth, so it's better if everybody gets along."

We have some graduates, too — people Pete and I used to work with who are no longer members of the Braves' broadcast team. The first of them was Darrel Chaney, who I thought was coming into his own as an announcer. He was a guy who asked everybody every day how he was doing and did everything anybody asked him to do — seemingly a perfect employee. Nobody ever said anything about Darrel except that he was doing a great job until they decided to fire him. It was a bitter pill for all of us, and I'm glad to say he's doing well in Atlanta in the real estate business.

Next came John Sterling. Alex Hawkins once said of Sterling, "John is too smart to be a sports announcer." Alex may have been right, but John was a million laughs to work with. He is one of those people who looks at life just a little bit differently than most of us. John once had a producer/director chide him for something he had said. Said the producer, "John, think." To which John replied, "I don't think, I just talk." Perhaps the perfect definition of what our job is. John is one of those guys who talks to himself when he's upset. At one time or another he has talked to every ticker-tape machine in baseball. But he's a helluva baseball and basketball announcer and is now the radio voice of the New York Yankees in his hometown.

Our other "graduate" is former outfielder Billy Sample, who is doing a good job broadcasting California Angels baseball these days. When Billy came to us he had never done any radio, yet they tried to make him a radio play-by-play man, and that is the toughest part of this job. He got better at it, but not quickly enough, and got let go. His TV analysis was fine, but the radio is what got him in Atlanta.

There are two unsung heroes in our operation. One works for television, one for radio. Hal Gaalema is our television statistician, and the man is a genius. A former college pitcher at South Carolina, he really knows the game, so he knows what stats to give you. Equally important, he doesn't try to sell you the stats he comes up with. If you don't use all his stuff, he doesn't sulk, and he's made all of us look a lot better than we are for a lot of years.

Then there's our radio producer/engineer Rick Shaw. Shaw is the most conscientious man I have ever been around. He handles the commercials, gets the game on the air, handles all the little bits of "business" the station has sold, and keeps us up-to-date on the out-of-town scores. He's been a loyal friend for a lot of years, and as the broadcast rights have seesawed between one station and another, he has somehow kept us from blowing any big accounts in the ever-changing world of radio. He is, bluntly, the best.

■　■　■

When Ted started us on the great adventure of cable television, beaming Braves games throughout the nation and beyond, a writer asked me what it was like. I said it was like being on the first wagon train heading west. You don't know where you're going exactly, and you don't know how it's going to come out, but you do know that you're having a helluva lot of fun trying to get there.

Years later I still feel that way, although I have a bone to pick with many of the journalists who now label themselves radio-television critics. The fact that none of these people understand how radio and television work doesn't give them the slightest pause as they pontificate on who does well and who does not. These fellows are sort of instant experts when some editor tells them they now cover the television sports beat. I think it's a severe indictment of our industry that we let some of these guys dictate to us what is good television and what is not.

One area in which I part company with most of these guys is in their misunderstanding of what we try to do on TBS when we televise 125 Braves games into people's homes each year. Here's what we do, and here's why we do it. What we do is, we root like hell for the Atlanta Braves to win every game that we televise. We don't keep that a secret; it's the way we do the games. Here's why we do it. Because if we didn't do it, we would be phonies.

Look, I get paid by the same people who pay Tom Glavine and David Justice. Of course I want them to do well. During the season you spend nearly as much time around the players, manager, and coaches as you do with your own family. You get to know mothers and fathers and brothers and sisters and children. If you did not root for those people, you would be a little bit bent.

And then there's the selfish side of things. When the Braves finish last, fewer people come to the park, fewer people watch on television, fewer people listen on radio, and less money comes into the company. Less money for the company means less money for the announcers the next time they have to negotiate their deals. Fewer people watching and listening means less likelihood that a sponsor is going to be doling out dollars to Skip Caray to do a commercial or two. You would have to be an idiot not to cheer for the team.

So we go on the air and try to be completely up-front about our allegiance. It drives some of those writers berserk. They seem to feel that we should *lie* to the public and pretend we don't care who wins. I refuse to do that.

You can root for the Braves and still be totally honest. If David Justice is in an 0-for-30 slump you have to report that, just as you have to report it when David Justice hits forty homers and drives in 120 runs. By the same token, if a guy like Barry Bonds comes into town and goes 15-for-20 against you, you give him all the credit in the world, even though he is breaking your heart. You can have a rooting interest and still be 100 percent honest. Many writers apparently don't understand that, although it doesn't seem that difficult to me.

I've seen the other side of the coin. I've broadcast NBA games and NFL games on our sister station TNT. If I had the Steelers against the Colts, I didn't care who won; I just hoped that the game would be a good one and that next week's game, say New England at Miami, would also be a good one. That is the big difference between the way we do baseball and the way the networks, including ESPN, do the games. Every game they do features two different teams, whereas the one constant in our telecasts is the Atlanta Braves. The ESPN guys and the ABC/NBC guys are absolutely right to do their games the way they do them, and the TBS, WGN and WWOR guys are absolutely right to do the games the way we do them.

One other point: We get a lot of mail during the course of the year. Much of it asks us to say happy birthday to someone, some of it is constructive criticism, and a good deal of it is praise for the way we do the games. But the letters that mean the most to me have come from Reds fans and Dodgers fans and Giants fans who have watched our telecast on nights when their own announcers aren't televising the game and have written to thank us for the fair way we treat their players. We feel like that's the way we are supposed to do it and that if we did it any other way we would be lying to our viewers, and that is the one thing my daddy taught me never to do.

I've had a lot of fun with my Braves allegiance. Out in San Francisco during the great pennant stretch drive of 1993 I was known as "the voice of evil" to Giants fans, thanks to a writer friend of mine out there named Ray Ratto. Whenever we would go to Candlestick, I'd hear about it from some of the fans, but I can honestly say it was all good natured. I think those good Giants fans knew where I was coming from and understood I was simply being honest about my feelings. They liked to needle me about my Braves affiliation, but they did it with grudging admiration.

I'll say it again. If Ralph Kiner and Tim McCarver and Gary

Thorne didn't have a rooting interest in the Mets, they would not be doing their jobs. If Harry Caray, Tom Brenneman, and Steve Stone did not have a rooting interest in the Cubs, they wouldn't be doing their jobs. If Pete Van Wieren, Don Sutton, Joe Simpson, and Skip Caray didn't have a rooting interest in the Braves, we would not be doing our jobs.

For the life of me I can't understand why the ink-stained wretches can't grasp this simple and fundamental concept. Am I wrong about this? I have asked myself that question on numerous occasions and I can say to you honestly that no, I am not wrong on this one. They are. So there.

■　■　■

The Braves are in Los Angeles in early 1994 and lefthander Kent Mercker hurls his first major league complete game. It also happens to be his first career shutout. It also happens to be a no-hitter against the powerful Dodgers.

I was working with Joe Simpson on this night, and he headed to the field in the ninth so that if Kent got the no-hitter, we could interview him live on TBS. Mercker got to our microphones while we

Kent Mercker being interviewed by Skip's son Chip Caray in 1992.
(Courtesy Turner Broadcasting System)

were still in the postgame commercial. He says to Joe with a huge smile on his face, "How lucky was that!" One of those potentially great television moments that circumstance dictated would never make the air; but what a nice moment to see a nice kid at his humblest.

And I'm not supposed to root for this team?

A final postscript on the no-hitter. The next day Mercker received a bottle of very good champagne from Pete Smith, the man whose spot Mercker had taken in the rotation. A class act from a class guy.

ASSORTED STORIES & ASIDES

ASK

SKIP

CARAY

I'm constantly asked how much prepara-tion it takes to get ready to do a major league baseball game. That's a tough one because, in a way, I've been preparing since I was about six years old.

I'm preparing every time I pick up the paper and turn to the sports page, but I don't think of it that way. I'm thinking that I am about to read about something I care deeply about. Every time I listen to a talk show, I'm trying to understand what the fans want to know so that I can provide it for them. I subscribe to *Baseball America* and *Sports Illustrated* not to get prepared to broadcast, but because I enjoy reading about the people involved in the game of baseball.

Our group of announcers usually arrives at the ballpark between 4:00 p.m. and 5:00 p.m. for a 7:40 game. Pete gets there first; Don and I tie for last with Joe in the middle. Even then, saying hello to the players and writers and coaches and other broadcasters, you are really having more fun than you are thinking about the upcoming game.

Some announcers really pore over the statistic sheets. I try not to, because when you do, you run the risk of using too many of them. I keep track of who has a hitting streak, who is red hot and who is ice cold, and that's about it. It seems to me that if you know the game of baseball, you're much more likely to be over-prepared than under-prepared. What we do every night, however, is gather over dinner in the press room and talk. We talk of our families; we talk of current events; and we talk about baseball each and every night. Again, it isn't a production meeting — it's something we all enjoy and a common bond that brings us together.

■ ■ ■

I also receive letter after letter asking how to get started on the road to becoming an announcer. With so many former players now in the booth, it ain't getting any easier. The odds against making it to the big leagues are tremendously long ones. But if you have that fire in your belly, if what we do is what you really want to do, I can offer a little advice.

First, take all the English courses you can and force yourself to read as much as possible. The more you read, the more comfortable with word usage you will be. And really, broadcasting is all about using language effectively.

Next, don't be afraid to work. Take a cheap little tape recorder and go to a ballpark in your home town and broadcast a game. Professional or high school — it doesn't matter. Listen to your first broadcast objectively. You will probably find fault to the point of despair. But remember that almost nobody likes how they sound on the air — so your first effort was probably only half as bad as you think it was. Take notes about what you didn't like about your work. Think about it and then go out and do it again and again and again. If you don't see any improvement, you may be barking up the wrong tree. But I can't overemphasize the importance of this kind of practice. And if sitting at a game blabbering into a tape recorder while your friends and perfect strangers stare and laugh at you is too humiliating for you, then forget about it. You won't make it in this business.

One thing you must have to do radio broadcasts is the God-given ability to see something and communicate that sight *quickly* from the eye through the brain to the mouth. This is a gift. I know a lot of people who are far more intelligent than am I who can't communicate quickly. That knocks you out of the radio business, but in television these days you don't have to be that quick.

Another reason it's very difficult to get work in the major leagues is that those of us fortunate enough to be here try to hang on for a long time. Look at my dad in Chicago, Vin Scully in Los Angeles, Jack Buck in St. Louis, Ernie Harwell in Detroit. They have been around a long, long time. It doesn't seem possible, but Pete and I are in our nineteenth year together with the Braves, and I feel I'm just getting started.

One final word of advice: never forget who you work for. And who you work for is not really the man who pays you. You don't work for the team and you don't work for the players. You work for the fan. On radio you are his eyes. On television you try to add information to make his viewing of the game a little more pleasurable. When

Man at work.

I'm broadcasting on radio, I always think of a cross country truck-
er hauling his load late at night and trying to listen to the game to
stay awake. My plan is to make it interesting and exciting enough
for him to complete his trip in safety. That might sound silly and

it probably is, but it's the image I have in my mind every time I grab a radio microphone.

Furthermore, working for the fan means being obligated to tell the truth and not sugarcoat the pill. If you don't respect the fan's intelligence, you will lose him for yourself and for your employer. I'm very fortunate to work for a man who gives his announcers the freedom to tell the unvarnished truth all the time. In the long run, honesty is helpful to everybody, but some owners and some announcers don't see it that way.

You also have to understand that you can't please everybody. Every time you open your mouth, you are going to make somebody angry — especially in this era of political correctness. But if all you say is "ball one" and "strike two," you are going to put your audience to sleep. There is a fine line between inducing boredom and overdoing it, and each announcer has to find it for himself. Which brings me to another point: be yourself. As a young announcer, I loved my dad to death, but I was so concerned about nepotism that I deliberately tried to *not* sound like him. I was worried so much about not sounding like Dad that I wasn't worrying enough about what I was saying.

People always ask me about my style. I don't have a style. I just see it, then I say it. If you try to sound unlike or like another announcer, you are doomed to failure. Just see it, say it, and hope for the best.

■　■　■

I've been asked about a million times which I prefer — television or radio — and people always seem surprised when I tell them that radio is my favorite. The reason is pretty simple, really. In radio your job is to paint the picture for the fan. You are his eyes when it comes to "watching" the action. In television, of course, the picture is already there, and your job is to try to fill in around the edges a little bit. And in television so many people are contributing to the broadcast that it sometimes gets a little unnerving. In radio it's just me and our producer/engineer Rick Shaw.

People from my generation grew up in the radio business and had to try to make the transition into television. Younger announcers — guys in their thirties and forties now — grew up in television and have to make the transition to radio, which is a good deal harder to do. I've seen some good television announcers fail miserably in radio.

As for me, I got into television by lying. When Tom Cousins and Carl Sanders bought the Hawks, they hired me to be the broadcaster and then asked me if I had done any television play-by-play. I said I had and then learned as I went. It worked out okay, and when I fessed up years later they both had a good laugh over it.

The hardest thing for any announcer trained in radio is to remember that the picture is there on TV and keep quiet. It is my sincere opinion that all of us talk too much on television. It's bad enough with two announcers, but when you cram three men into the booth like they do on "Monday Night Football" over at ABC, it gets a little ridiculous. It isn't the fault of any one announcer. You figure you have to protect your job by saying as much as the guy next to you, so when it's a trio, the whole thing just gets out of hand.

Another reason radio is more fun is that you don't have to bother with replays and the like. They are a valuable tool in television, although at times I think they are overused. Ours is a wonderful business, but sometimes I think the television producers and directors tend to direct the game for their peers and their bosses rather than taking into consideration what the fans wants to see and hear. Some guys work so hard on their thirty-second tease and their two-minute on-camera open that they have the crew exhausted by the time the game gets underway. And once it starts, they have no logical plan on how to proceed. Less and less do they think of the game as a whole — the thing the fans have tuned in in the first place.

■　■　■

You have to be careful what you say on both radio and TV because some folks take you so literally. I remember Ernie used to always say after the first four and a half innings, "We're going to leave you now and go to Braves Radio." An irate lady called the office one day complaining that it was ridiculous that only half the game was on television and half on radio. She understood that Ernie was leaving, but she didn't realize that either Pete or myself was heading toward the TV booth to take Ernie's place.

Another lady from out in Oregon called me one day demanding to know where she could purchase a Braves radio so she could hear the games that were not televised. She had heard me say, "No TV tomorrow, but we'll have it for you on Braves Radio at 7:35." I had to explain to her that there was no such thing as a Braves radio and that, even if there was, it couldn't be heard all the way out in Oregon. I had a difficult time convincing her.

During the 1993 season the Braves had a roadtrip from hell. We went from Atlanta to San Francisco, San Francisco to Miami, Miami to St. Louis, St. Louis to Atlanta. On the San Francisco portion of the trip, I mentioned that the Braves would be flying over Atlanta at about 3:30 a.m. and that it would be great if the fans went out into their backyards and waved to us with their flashlights as we flew over. I said they could repeat the procedure during our flight from Miami to St. Louis. Several people called the Braves' office trying to get precise times for our trips so they could do what I had kiddingly suggested. The long-suffering switchboard operators, whose lives I have made hell for many many years, had to report that it was just a little more Skip stupidity.

■　■　■

Speaking of phone calls, it was one of my crazy stunts that helped convince the citizenry of Atlanta that Ted Turner's cable-television scheme was actually going to work. Early on in the days when TBS started doing the games, things were a little grim. It was early in the year. The team was bad and the weather was lousy. Nobody was coming to the games.

Some genius at the *Atlanta Constitution* got the bright idea of calling ten people at random. *None* of the ten people the paper reached was watching the game. From that bit of in-depth research came a headline reading something like: "Nobody watching Braves at stadium or at home." It was the kind of publicity that causes advertisers to cancel their sponsorship of your broadcasts.

I took a calculated chance the night that headline appeared. On-air I read the headline and the story below it about how nobody cared that the Braves were on television at all, much less cable television. Then I gave out the number of the *Constitution* sports department and suggested that, in the off chance that *somebody* might be watching by accident, maybe they should give the paper a call and let them know.

It was wonderful. It was beyond my wildest dreams. We blew out their switchboard in about two minutes, and I finally had to beg the fans to stop because the phone load was so great it was running over into other exchanges, including the one for Grady Hospital. They got calls for days — calls from Alaska, California, Nebraska, Puerto Rico, and just about everywhere else. To the newspaper's credit they ran a story the next day in which they expressed amazement at the number of people who were, in fact, watching Braves baseball. It was my one tiny contribution to Ted Turner's brilliant success, but I'm proud of that move even today. If nobody had called, of course, Mr. Turner would have doubtless found himself another announcer. As it was, I was a hero for a day. To those of you who called, thanks a million.

ROCKY ROAD TO WAR

Variety, the show business newspaper, carried a story on September 4, 1974, about my effort to cover a war. It was written by my colleague at the time, Ernie Weatherall, a freelance radio reporter for ABC News.

Here it is, all true and slightly understated:

(Ankara, Turkey, Sept. 3) It was for all bubbling girls like Sandy, who cooed, "Gee, it must be exciting to be a TV correspondent and travel all over the world doing stories," that I kept this log.

It covers the 36 hours I spent on the road with ABC News' man in Bonn, West Germany, Don Farmer, cameraman Vincent Gaito, and soundman Teddy John, along with the star of the team — 500 pounds of cameras, lights and sound equipment and other excess baggage.

[The log begins:]

All Turkish airports closed because of the fighting in Cyprus. Farmer will make an end run into Turkey via Eastern Europe. We cover the last part of the journey via the Orient Express to Istanbul. Then to Ankara, hopefully then to Cyprus [which the Turks were invading at the time].

Flew from Frankfurt to Prague. However, Iraqi plane to Sofia, Bulgaria, not running for two days. Probably their flying rug salesman, who walks up and down the aisle during the flights, is ill.

Caught flight to Budapest. Wilted in stuffy, warm airport building. Secret police keep an eye on us. Try to get some fresh air outside but police say no.

A communist Zsa Zsa Gabor airline girl says we must have a visa to get outside building. The cost: $13. Says it will take an hour to get a visa. By that time our plane leaves. We decide to suffer and mutter.

Got seats on Balkan Airlines to Sofia. Given first-class seats in tiny compartment. Suspect it was to keep us decadent capitalists away from the proletariat. Stewardess gives us bottle of Russian vodka and goat cheese on black bread for snacks.

A little crowded on the Russian-made airliner. One stewardess sits on the sink in the pantry on takeoff, her hefty legs up against galley cabinets to hold them closed. We try small talk.

She says something in Bulgarian, the drift of which was "Drink your vodka and shut up."

Missed the Orient Express train in Sofia so we took two taxis to the Turkish border. Small loss. The train is neither an express, nor does it go to the Orient.

One of our taxis — Russian "Volgas" dating back to Stalin's time — breaks down at night on deserted road. Driver crawls under the car with flaming torch looking for the trouble. We flee to the countryside.

Twenty kilometers from the border, we are stopped by Bulgarian police. Foreigners not allowed any closer. We wave an old receipt, shouting, "This is a pass from Comrade Lenin himself." They are not amused.

Spend cold, hungry night in cabs. Very depressed when we hear on BBC radio that there is a cease-fire on Cyprus. Our trip is in vain. We open our last emergency ration, a bottle of Scotch bought at the duty-free shop in Frankfurt 2000 years ago.

Officer comes to escort us to Turkish border. We are dumped out at checkpoint. Bulgarians debate whether to confiscate our equipment which they say was brought in illegally. Problem solved when we meet a Bulgarian who has a cousin in Chicago.

Find bus carrying Turkish workers in Germany back to the homeland for vacation. They welcome us aboard. One problem: they must finish making a part for the engine of their ancient bus before it will start. Two hours later, we're on our way.

Bus smells of stale beer, goat cheese, Turkish tobacco, and unwashed socks. But who cares? The workers are friendly. We all speak to each other in fractured German.

Istanbul, at last. We switch ourselves and equipment to rented minibus with driver when the Turkish workers' bus reaches its destination on outskirts of town.

The new driver, whom we call Ghengis, immediately smashes into the back of a parked car. Driver of damaged car snatches keys of minibus. We have to pay him $160 for damages before we get keys back. How are we going to explain that on the expense account?

Ghengis cannot find the Istanbul Hilton. We end up in a red light district. The girls look at us and think it's raining dollars from heaven. Finally we find the hotel.

Our leader, Don Farmer, is afraid we look so crummy that the hotel will banish us back to bordello row.

As we register at the front desk, a correspondent from another network comes out of the elevator. He is cool, clean, and arrogant, as usual.

"Did you just get back from the front?" he asks, as though he has smelled something bad.

We tell him of our odyssey.

"But the airport at Istanbul opened this morning," he tells us. "I just flew in from London."

We hate him.

Worse, the Turks refused to let us cover their occupation of Cyprus. We had to fly to Athens, then to Nicosia, Cyprus, to cover the war from the Greek side. But the fighting was over. We hated that, too.

JERKS

When you televise a couple hundred sports events a year, your face gets on camera a lot, which makes you what I call a psuedo-celebrity. It's not that you do anything thrilling like the athletes you cover, but because you cover them, your face gets recognized. The large majority of people who do recognize you are unfailingly nice and supportive. Of course, human nature being what it is, you take the good people for granted and only tend to remember the jerks.

Two things I really hate. One is when people come up to me and say, "Gee, I think you're great. You're a lot better than your father." Not only is it not true, but what would those same people do if I said something to insult their fathers?

The second happens when a fan who recognizes me is accompanied by someone who doesn't. They approach me — invariably in a crowded place — and the fan starts pointing at me and exclaiming at the top of his voice, "Do you know who this is?" Now not only is his friend staring at me, but so is everybody else in the restaurant or the supermarket. Naturally, his friend doesn't know Skip Caray from Michael Jackson, which is embarrassing to his friend and embarrassing to me. All you can do is grin and bear it — but inside you'd love to pop the guy just to see what would happen.

MY ALL-TIMER OCCURRED BACK in 1981. Our son Josh was born more than two months prematurely and was in the intensive care ward for the first seven weeks of his life. His breathing stopped several times, but thanks to the wonderful people at Northside Hospital, he made it. Still, it was an incredibly stressful time, both for me and Paula. I was trying to raise the other kids, do my job, and spend time at the hospital just like any other father would do.

Josh's doctor told me the day I was bringing Paula home that his chances were no better than fifty-fifty. I was standing in line to pay her hospital bill and trying to figure out whether or not to tell her the distressing news. She's a tough lady, but she'd been through an awful lot. The guy behind me in line recognized me and asked me a question about the previous night's game, which I answered to the best of my ability. He asked me another question, and I replied, "I'm sorry, sir, but I really don't want to talk about baseball right now."

That was the end of our conversation. I paid the hospital bill, took my wife home and, thank God, son Joshua pulled through just fine. So fine in fact that a week or so later I rejoined the Braves on a West Coast roadtrip. Back home, I was checking my mail, and one of the first pieces I saw was an inter-office envelope from Ted Turner. I opened it and saw a letter. It was from the guy who had stood behind me in line at the hospital. He demanded that Ted fire me because I was rude to him when he asked about the Braves. Turner had scrawled, "What's this about?" across the top of the letter.

I didn't respond to Turner. Instead, I responded to the letter, calling that poor jerk every name I could think of. We were in a hospital, not a barroom. How could anyone be so inconsiderate? He never answered my letter, but I sent a copy to Turner. It was the most vicious letter I've ever written. After reading it, Turner sent it back to me again with his characteristic scrawl saying, "Good for you. Glad all is well." Another reason I like the guy.

It's probably not fair to bring up these examples of fans' rudeness. As I said, by and large they are wonderful. They also pay my salary, and I'm well aware of that. But there are some people who will drive you to the wall.

EYEWASH

ON THE

ROCKS

One night in 1984, after a Braves game, Skip and I got together for a few drinks and ended up in a late-night bar. It stays open until 4:00 a.m., which was almost what it was when we had the run-in with a drunken customer. Skip and I were sitting in the almost deserted bar, talking quietly. From across the room a guy in his twenties barked, "Hey, are you Skip Caray?"

Skip nodded and turned back to our conversation. The guy kept talking, loudly, slurring his words in the time-honored tradition of 3:45 a.m. drunks.

"Hey, Caray, those guys'll never win another pennant, ya know?" he slurred.

Skip looked over, frowned, then ignored the guy. But Mr. Seven-and-Seven would not be deterred: "You oughta tell the truth on TV, man," he said, not noticing that Skip's face was getting red.

Even in the dim light of that bar, designed to erase wrinkles and other ravages of time and strong drink, I could see the blood rising.

"Yeah, right. Look, we're talking here, OK?" Skip said to the man with the glazed eyes.

"Yeah, well I'm talking to you, man," the drunk responded and walked over to where we were sitting.

The bartender came over. I told him to try to keep the drunk away from us.

"Just offer to buy him a drink," the bartender told me, "and I'll take care of it."

This bartender was a veteran at handling drunks. He didn't want an angry Skip Caray on his hands, and he didn't want some guy decked by a celebrity, or vice-versa. So he came up with a novel "solution."

"Hey, Jerry, buy this guy a drink," I said, a little too loud, knowing that in the drunk's current condition, a Sex Pistols concert might not be loud enough to vibrate his eardrums.

The guy was surprised, but managed to mumble something about Seven-and-Seven. Then he turned back to Skip, in his face now, and muttered, "You're just a bunch of phonies."

"Enjoy your drink and please leave us alone," I said, watching Skip's patience wear thin.

The drunk gulped his drink, blinked a couple of times, sat down on a stool next to Skip and started to say something. Suddenly, beads of sweat began to break out on his forehead. He frowned, got off the stool, and headed toward the men's room at the back of the club. He moved faster as he got closer to the rest room door.

He pushed open the door, dashed in, and didn't come out for about ten minutes. When he did surface, he was white as whipped cream, shaking a little, and subdued a lot. Without a word to us or to the bartender, the pale young man, minus his attitude, walked out of the bar.

Skip was impressed and I was relieved. I already had been imagining the headlines in the next day's paper — *"Braves announcer beats up young man half his size in barroom brawl."*

The bartender, whose secret I'm about to reveal and whose name is not really Jerry, just smiled and threw away the rest of that guy's drink.

"What did you do?" I asked.

"Well, we didn't want a scene, right? We didn't want a fight, right? And we didn't want to throw him out and have him make up lies about Skip Caray's bodyguards or something, right?"

"Yeah, right," said Skip, "but what did you do?"

The bartender leaned in and said just above a whisper, "Eyewash."

"What?"

"Eyewash," he repeated. "A couple of drops of eyewash in a drink will make you sick in a couple of minutes." He showed us the little plastic dispenser bottle in his pocket.

Apparently, it gets more than the red out. It takes dinner and maybe lunch out as well. We laughed, amazed at this simple solution.

"And the beauty of it is, it makes the drunk throw up, feel lousy, want to go home to bed, and it has no aftereffects," Jerry said.

I have told this story to a few other select bartenders over the years and none of them has heard of using eyewash as a means of controlling drunks. So I'm not positive that Jerry told me the truth about what he put in that guy's drink. Skip said we should try it sometime to see if it works.

We keep forgetting to do that.

**AND
ROUNDING
OUT OUR
CREW . . .**

Our long-suffering television producer Glenn Diamond and his beautiful wife Nancy were returning from a roadtrip. It was about 8:30 on a busy Sunday night in Hartsfield International Airport in Atlanta. Accompanying the Diamonds on their trip to the busy concourse were director Tom Smith, statistician Hal Gaalema, and one portly baseball announcer. Bugging producers has been my hobby for several years, and this night offered a better target of opportunity than usual. Lovely Nancy, you see, was very obviously seven months pregnant. She and Glenn got on the people mover. I trotted (okay, waddled) alongside, imploring Nancy at the top of my lungs to leave Glenn and live with me. I claimed, of course, that the child was mine. Smith and Gaalema were in hysterics, Nancy was hissing, "Shut up, Skip," and Glenn was just shaking his head in resignation. You have to like people a lot to put them through something like that . . . and they have to like you.

Back to my habit of bugging producers. When I first started televising Atlanta Hawks basketball back in the late 1960s, there was no such thing as a producer. We didn't even travel with a director. When the Hawks had a game on the road, I would drive by the station, pick up the format (a list of the commercials to be run during the game and the length of each), and then I would head for the airport. When I got to the game a television director would sidle up to me. I'd give him the format, then he'd say something like, "How ya wanna do this?" I'd reply, "You try to follow what I say and I'll try to follow what you shoot, and we'll probably end up alright." And we did.

It was those days that got me started in television. I was my own producer and didn't even know it. In short, I made all the decisions and suffered the consequences, both good and bad, that resulted from those decisions. Having that kind of responsibility for several years, if nothing else, makes you self-reliant. If you don't get fired along the way, you get pretty confident that you

Producer Glenn Diamond with Pete, Skip, and Don.
(Courtesy Turner Broadcasting System)

know what you're doing and what works best.

Eventually, our own director began to travel along. Taking a director on the road was a step forward for the whole telecast — *if* the
director knew what he was doing. I really don't know when producers came along. It seemed that I looked up one day in the late
'70s or early '80s, and there was Glenn Diamond shaking my hand
and saying, "Hi, I'm your producer."

Producers do serve a purpose. They are especially important
when you have announcers who blow dry their hair and know almost
nothing about the sport they are covering. Those guys need a producer to cover a vulnerable part of their anatomy. Of course,
when you have been successful doing it your way and suddenly
somebody is trying to make you do it *his* way, there are going to
be problems.

Most of the problems for me came during basketball broadcasts when TNT first started doing NBA games. I was assigned a
producer who shall remain nameless. He had never produced anything before; he had been a unit manager at one of the networks.
He was an old buddy of one of my bosses, and he needed the job.

The fact that he knew nothing about basketball and even less about television was apparently not important.

One night I was doing a Boston-Houston game in the old Boston Garden. Ralph Sampson was injured in the game, and it looked like it might be a bad one. I sent my analyst, John Andariese, to find the Boston team doctor, and John managed to bring him by the table. I interviewed him while the game was going on, knowing that we had a big story. I pulled off my headset and held just the microphone portion between us to do the interview. He announced that while Sampson was indeed hurt he would be okay to play within two or three weeks. We had a major scoop.

What was my producer doing? Nothing until after the game when he told me it didn't look good to hold a headset like that. After I suggested to him that he perform a feat upon himself that would have been physically impossible, I decided that I would just keep doing the games my way and that if the people who employed me didn't like it they could always get another announcer. So far so good for me. What started so contrarily has actually turned into a very good working relationship. There are times the producers drive me crazy, but God knows there are times when I drive *them* crazy, so it all works out about even.

I think our crew is the best in baseball and for a very simple reason. Our guys televise about 125 games for us each year. They've been at it for a long time and they take great pride in their work. It's only natural to improve by repetition, and our guys have gotten to the point where they could do it in their sleep if they had to. It's a great pleasure to walk into the ballpark each night knowing you're going to be working with the very best. Network camera people get to work maybe twenty games a year. They can't carry our guys' TelePrompters.

■ ■ ■

I do maintain, though, that when things go wrong with a broadcast, often it is the producers and the technical people who are to blame. I read the other day that sixteen cameras were going to be used to televise the Stanley Cup Finals. I knew immediately that would be a mucked-up telecast. Why? Because when a director and a producer have that many cameras at their disposal, they feel compelled to use them to justify the expense of setting them up and crewing them. Suddenly the thrills on the ice are secondary to the people in the truck. That is also why so many Super Bowls and World Series are poorly televised. I wish more people in our business agreed with the wise maxim, "If it ain't broke, don't fix it."

Also, any producer who misses a pitch in baseball to show a third replay of anything should immediately be fired. We have an obligation to our viewer to show him the game. Replays can come later or not at all. To miss a pitch used to be a near-criminal offense. Now it is almost routine. I yearn for the good old days which, I guess, is another sign that I am turning into an old codger.

WHAT'S SO FUNNY?

One of my favorite places on a weekend is the press room before a Braves game at Atlanta Fulton County Stadium. It's a place where reporters and other media people hang out to get a cheap buffet lunch and to pick up the latest statistics on the Braves and their opponents that day.

The press lounge is behind the wall that runs along the back of the press box and the broadcast booths. It attracts hordes of media types during playoffs and World Series games, but on a routine Sunday afternoon at mid-season, it's a casual, low-key place.

Most of the people there are working or getting ready to, but there's time for the normal bull sessions that accompany any sporting event. Chris and I usually stop in there to see Skip and other friends on the Braves broadcast team — Don Sutton, Pete Van Wieren and Joe Simpson. We get the important stuff out of the way first — the new jokes, or even recycled ones if we can find an unwary soul who hasn't heard them.

I learned a long time ago that the raunchy jokes that pepper newsrooms around the world are no match for the X-rated laughers the sports guys tell each other. On that bright Sunday afternoon, waiting for game-time, Don Sutton had a fresh cache of jokes that turned the air blue. This one was Don's cleanest of the day:

"So Skip and I are walking down the street the other day, and on the corner we see a very young hooker.

"We walk up to her, and Skip says, 'Young lady, this is not right. You shouldn't be here. Do you know how mad your mother would be if she knew you were standing here soliciting for sex on this corner right now?'

"Replied the hooker, 'Yes, I do. She'd be mad alright, because this is her corner.'"

We all laughed, and I filed it under "jokes I can repeat in places other than prison." Most of Sutton's jokes are more appropriate for use as ice-breakers at an execution.

As the Braves ran onto the field to begin the ball game that Sunday afternoon, Chris and I went to our seats, slightly below and to the right of the Braves radio broadcast booth.

We strapped on our headset radios and tuned in Skip and Don, who began the game on radio that day. In the second inning, Skip got our attention as he told his radio audience: "We have some local celebrities in the stands today—from WSB-TV, news anchors Chris Curle and Don Farmer. Always nice to see them here at the old ballpark, that married couple that does the news."

Then Don said to Skip and everyone else listening on the Braves radio network: "I wonder how Don and Chris met?"

Replied Skip, "Well, Don, I don't know, maybe on a street corner."

"I'll bet Don asked Chris how her Mom felt about them meeting like that," said Sutton, starting to giggle. "And Chris probably said, 'She'd be mad alright, because this is her corner.'"

Skip laughed and Don laughed. Chris and I turned in our seats, looked up at the radio booth, and laughed back at them. They grinned and snickered through the next at bat and into a commercial at the end of the inning.

A couple of other fans sitting near us who had radios tuned to the game looked at us, puzzled. And a lot of people in the radio audience probably wondered what the hell was so funny.

MAKING HAY AT WXIA

One part of my life I am not so proud of was when I was sports director of what is now WXIA TV in Atlanta. In those days they only did an eleven o'clock news show, which wasn't good news for me. I was between marriages and hitting the streets about as hard as it is humanly possible to hit them. A six o'clock news hour would have slowed me down. The eleven o'clock was an adventure for me every night.

My buddy (and now fellow sportscaster) Bob Neal was the news director, and a very lovely lady named Linda Faye was our weathercaster. The two of them were great friends to me, and our ratings were really quite good. Some strange things happened, however, primarily because I didn't feel that sobriety was a necessity when doing the sports.

I perspire a good bit — and the booze and the TV lights made it worse. Every night I came on the air looking like Albert Brooks in *Broadcast News*. I recall one night when a fly landed on my nose right in the middle of the sports. I introduced him as "Herbert, our studio fly." Then I flicked him away and told him to come back in one minute. Honest to God, about a minute later the fly landed on my nose again. The crew was in hysterics, and so was I. It may have been the funniest thing I've ever been involved in in the television business — being upstaged by an insect.

■ ■ ■

Our general manager in those days was a delightful man named George Hager. One day he called me into his office and told me we had a problem. His station had the wrestling programming in Atlanta, and wrestling was then, as it is now, a tremendous moneymaker. Every Friday when it was time to give the results, I always made fun of it, calling it what it was — an exhibition, not a sport. It's fake, folks — trust me.

In any event, Mr. Hager was getting heat from the wrestling promoters, who were threatening to move their "sport" to another station if I didn't stop telling the truth about them. I reminded

George that when he put me on the air he told me to tell it like it is, and I told him there was no way I would pretend wrestling was legitimate. I was young and feisty in those days, and I felt (and still feel) that if you don't have your integrity you don't have much of anything. We finally reached a compromise. I wouldn't do the wrestling anymore; Linda would do it — thus saving my reputation.

Linda didn't know if wrestling was fake or not and didn't care. We thought the problem was solved, and it would have been except for my big mouth. This was in the days of "happy talk" news where the anchors made small talk as they passed the baton from news to weather to sports and then back to news. When it came Linda's time to introduce the sports she turned to me and brightly said, "Well, Skip, tonight I know something about sports that you don't. I know the wrestling results."

Without thinking I replied, "I know 'em, too, Linda; I saw the rehearsal. But why don't you tell the rest of the people." Wrestling soon went to a competitive station then named WTCG. You may have heard of it. It's now called TBS. That was the start of my demise at Channel 11, and the final blow was also self-inflicted.

■　■　■

I have a very dear friend named Frank Hyland, a fine sportswriter for many years with the *Atlanta Journal*. Frank and I, in our younger days, were soulmates. We married at about the same time in our lives; we each fathered two children; and we got divorced at about the same time. Footloose and fancy free, we were taken by the bright lights of the city and were especially enamored of a place (now defunct) called the Braves-Falcon Lounge.

The Braves-Falcon was the last tavern before you commuted into then dry DeKalb County in suburban Atlanta. Enough folks stopped by for "one for the road" that the Braves-Falcon became the first million-dollar bar in Atlanta, I am told. I don't know about a million, but Hyland and I made regular contributions to the place — to the point that I used to get some of my mail delivered there.

One day right before Christmas Hyland and I hooked up at about eleven o'clock in the morning. There were Christmas parties all over town, and I'm rather afraid we set a new world record for parties attended and adult beverages consumed. The last and best party of the night was at the Braves-Falcon, where we not only celebrated the holiday season, but met up with two young lovelies who were ready for action.

At about 10:15 p.m., the bartender, a buddy named Dick Norton, tapped me on the shoulder and said, "Skip, don't you have a television show to do in about forty-five minutes?" Sadly, the answer was yes. I switched to coffee, but after eleven hours of competitive drinking, the term "too little too late" came into play.

I had no time to prepare a television show, so I had a brainstorm. I'd have Hyland on as my guest. The NFL playoffs were scheduled for the weekend, and Hyland was the beat writer covering the Atlanta Falcons. I figured we could bluff it, and the two ladies said they'd just love to see a real television station and a real star like myself in action. Yeah.

Honest to God, I was okay. I wasn't great, but I had done this before, and knew I could vamp my way through it. Hyland seemed fine, too, until they turned the lights on. Then he began listing to port a bit in his chair.

"Frank," says I, "who do you like in the Dallas game tomorrow?"

"Who are they playing?" was his reply.

"Kansas City," stated yours truly with only a slight lisp.

"Who cares?" said Hyland, almost falling off his chair.

"Who let this guy in here?" said I. It was the shortest sports segment in the history of television. It was also my last, and deservedly so. Hager called me the next day and explained that his boss was in town and he had been bragging all through dinner about what a great find he had as a sportscaster. I got myself fired and I damn near got Hager fired.

I will say this, though. If everybody saw that show who claims he saw that show, they should have kept me on because the ratings must have been through the roof. It's one I'll never live down, and it's one I'm not proud of, but, God, it was funny. I learned a valuable lesson there. Booze and broadcasting do not mix — at least until after the game or after the show.

The ladies, by the way, were not impressed. No hits, no runs, no errors and absolutely nobody left.

SAVING GRACE

CHRIS

Senator Bob Dole once told me, on television in a live interview, that he and I both had "over-married." It was a compliment to my wife and to his, Elizabeth Dole. My wife is Chris Curle, whom he liked a lot better than he did me. He knew she was a TV person and he enjoyed her work.

Chris and I have been in the same business — TV News — all our professional lives, and that has presented some, uh, challenges. Sometimes people think that because we are married and on television, we are therefore always together.

One evening several years ago, Charlton Heston and Ted Turner, my friend and former boss, were the MCs of the world premier of the movie *The Right Stuff* at the Fox Theater in Atlanta. Chris and I were invited to the premier and the dinner dance afterward at the High Museum.

I was in the men's room at the Fox when Ted came in.

"Hi, Don. Where's Chris, why isn't she with you?" he said as he sidled up to a nearby urinal.

I explained that, since we were in the men's room, Chris probably wouldn't be expected to be there.

"She's in the lady's room, Ted," I said.

"Oh well, tell her I'm sorry I missed her," said Ted. He then asked me why I was wearing a tux. I mentioned the fact that the event was black tie and that he was an MC. He was wearing old, brown, scuffed shoes, a rumpled sport coat, and a frown.

"Oh, should I be dressed like that?" he asked, disdainful of my penguin look.

"Ted, you can dress any way you like," I grinned. I was right. He can.

Ted usually thought of Chris and me as the same person, or at least as two people who had no lives before each other. That's not totally true. Chris and I met at a riot. It was a small-scale riot, by present standards, but a violent demonstration nevertheless, a news event that we both were covering in Houston. Chris worked for a TV station there, and I was in Houston doing a long story on race relations in education for ABC News.

A group of Hispanic parents — and some others, as well — were angry about something the Houston school board had done. When the vote went against them at the board meeting, the people began running through the halls of the building, breaking things and hollering.

I had already seen Chris in the newsroom of her TV station; it was an ABC affiliate and I was using it as a base of operations. That night, when the school board meeting erupted, I was running with my cameraman down a hall, and Chris came running by with her cameraman.

On impulse, I shouted, "Hey, Chris, what are you doing after the riot?"

She grinned and said something like, "Nothing. Why?" But her words were lost in the commotion of our running off in opposite directions.

I assumed we had a date. As it turns out, we did.

■　■　■

Before I found Chris, I was living in a one-bedroom apartment in a complex that had more flight attendants than a fleet of jumbo jets. I was recently divorced, which means I was currently poor. I owned a car and some socks, but the furniture was rented, and most of my record albums were stolen by a girl I went out with a couple of times.

The night of the theft was our last date, of course, but there were so many single girls in Atlanta then that I bounced back quickly. The law of supply and demand is a wonderful law indeed, when they're in supply and you're in demand. The ratio of men to women then was so favorable to males that some dates actually brought records to my place, after I explained that mine had been liberated by another woman.

Skip was also recently divorced and having similar experiences in our new world of singlehood. Once we got over the trauma of divorce, we forced ourselves to wallow on the wild side of Single Atlanta. It was the heyday of male chauvinist pig-ism, and Skip and I were among the head hogs.

When my local heaven on earth was interrupted by an assignment in Vietnam, Skip immediately volunteered to sublet the apartment. It was a good deal for me financially; he paid the rent at Riverbend, including the leased furniture, while I was living off ABC News in a Quonset hut barracks in Quang Tri.

After the Vietnam stint and a trip home through Asia and Europe, I began dating Chris, who lived in Houston, Texas. I found that when I asked her to come to Atlanta for a weekend, my male friends were shocked.

"Man, you're importing a girl?" I'd hear. "Like there aren't enough here already?"

When Chris showed up, they were impressed, but they were still nervous about having her mingle with the single girls they dated in Atlanta. It was clear that they didn't want Chris's independence ruining a way of life the guys had spent years perfecting.

I moved from Riverbend soon after that and even bought some

Chris and Don accompanied by earlier incarnations of themselves — Chris as news anchor at ABC affiliate WJLA-TV in Washington, and Don as ABC News correspondent covering Capitol Hill.

furniture. In early '72, Chris and I married and moved to London. Skip had another couple of years of the Hotlanta life until Paula appeared and made all the rest of it seem irrelevant.

Occasionally we talk about those days. I compare that time to my assignment in Vietnam. I'm glad I did it, but I wouldn't ever want to do it again. Ever.

■   ■   ■

Even though we've spent our professional lives on TV, Chris and I do not have an Ozzie-and-Harriet marriage. She is a lot better looking than Harriet, for one thing. I am better dressed than Ozzie, for another. The public, however, has shown an occasional glimmer of interest in our lifestyles at home and elsewhere off the tube.

Most people assume that we spend every night at parties and every weekend at some glittery affair or out-of-town luxury spot. Ha!

When we lived in Washington, Chris was a local news anchor and better known to the public than I was. Her daily newscasts had a lot higher profile than did my two-minute report on the ABC News nightly half-hour.

She also worked harder, or at least longer days, and often didn't get home in the evening until 8:30 or so. Since I usually got home by 7:30, I became the cook. That was OK with me, but in adjusting to my role, I almost became the anal retentive Felix of *The Odd Couple* to Chris's role as Oscar.

It came to a head one evening in the winter of 1978. I got home about 7:15 p.m. and skinned a couple of chicken breasts, marinated them in olive oil and spices, and scrubbed a couple of potatoes. I used the microwave for the potatoes since I wanted them to be ready when Chris got home.

By 8:30, the chicken was done, the potatoes were ready, and the steamed broccoli was perfect. By 9:00, the chicken was dry, the potatoes were hard, and the broccoli was comatose. By 9:15, the dinner was ruined and I was in a snit.

Chris got home about 9:25. "Hi, honey. I'm home," she chirped as she came in the front door.

I walked to the foyer in my apron, an oven mitt on one hand, a large fork in the other.

"Do you know what time it is?" I asked, sounding more like a crazed Harriet than an affable Ozzie.

"Sure," she said, suppressing a grin at my appearance, a sort of cross between Julia Childs and Mr. Food.

"Well, it's 9:26, exactly. Where have you been?" I was out of control now, and just barely suppressing it.

"A bunch of us went for drinks after the show," she said, unaware of the gravity of her transgression.

"Well, don't they have phones in that bar?" I barked. "You could have called. The dinner is ruined and it's your fault!"

Chris stopped taking off her coat and looked at me.

What she saw was not her husband Don, the guy who covers the Congress for ABC News. No, she saw Satan with a blender, Lucifer with a "Kiss the Cook" apron, the Prince of Darkness with a wilted lettuce salad on the table.

Chris saved our marriage right then, at that very moment. She laughed.

Thank God she did. I believe her laughter was the only thing in the world that could have made me realize what I was saying and how I looked, standing there like a home economics class dropout. Then we both started laughing.

I poured the wine and she ordered a pizza.

We laugh about that evening now, and I'm even able to tell the story to others, as you can see.

Chris brings to television some of that special quality that allowed her to laugh us out of a domestic crisis that night back in 1978. That is, she takes her work seriously, but not herself. I guess that comes across on the tube, because so many people ask me so often, "Is Chris Curle half as nice in person as she is on television?"

I usually smile and say, "Oh yes, she's a sweetheart in real life as well."

And it's true. But one day some years ago, I had just about had enough of the Chris Curle fan club asking me about her. I was having a bad day anyway, and when the millionth person asked me, "Is Chris half as nice as she is on TV?" I snarled to the questioner, "Yes, she's exactly half as nice."

PAULA &
JOSH

Twenty years ago I was a moderately successful, mostly unhappy character. I was divorced, and my kids, Chip and Cindy, lived 600 miles away in St. Louis. I missed them dreadfully and spent my life on the streets. Then I met Paula. Actually she had been my barber/hairdresser/cosmetologist for a couple of years before we dated. That's probably the best way — become friends first, then become romantically involved. We have been married for a long time now, and it's been absolutely wonderful. She's a strong, loyal, and beautiful lady, and I can't imagine how crummy my life would be without her.

Then there's Josh, our twelve-year-old son. I wasn't around as much as I should have been when Chip and Cindy and Shayelyn (Paula's daughter whom I adopted) were growing up. I was doing both basketball and baseball and was never home. I'll regret that till my dying day, but when you are young and trying to get ahead, you do things to succeed professionally that aren't always good for your family life. When Josh came along, I realized I had

Skip, Paula, and Josh enjoy a family outing.

Skip, Josh, and Chip at spring training in 1991.
(Courtesy Turner Broadcasting System)

my last chance to be a real father. I don't know how well I'm doing at fatherhood, but he's a wonderful boy and the joy of my life these days. I wish for everyone else the warm feeling I have each time I head into my driveway. I hope everybody loves going home as much as I. My other kids, Chip, Cindy, and Shayelyn, turned out fine. I just wish I had been around more while they were growing up.

I guess what I'm trying to say is, I'm a pretty lucky guy. I have an exciting job and a wonderful family. To my family and to those of you who watch and listen to the Braves, my deep and sincere thanks. It's all of you who have blessed me with good fortune.

the ROAST

I t's a tradition that we roast the ones we love, but tonight, we are breaking that tradition."

That comment by Stan Kasten, the president of the Atlanta Braves and the Atlanta Hawks, spiced a roast of my roomie, my pal, Skip Caray, on May 23, 1994.

Hundreds of people paid $100 a plate to hear Skip's friends and coworkers skewer him to raise money for Camp Twin Lakes, a camp for chronically ill children. It's one of Skip's favorite causes and he serves on the board.

Braves announcer Don Sutton was a masterful master of ceremonies. His announcing partner Joe Simpson did a funny imitation of Carnac the Magnificent, with Skip the butt of his jokes.

For about ninety minutes, Skip got an earful about his foibles and frailties from a bunch of us who would rather be the roasters than the roastees. These comments from his "friends" show why.

■ Ernie Johnson, retired Braves announcer: "Skip is getting on in years, as his buddy Jiggs McDonald (a hockey announcer) found out in New York one night.

"Skip and Jiggs were returning to their hotel after a long night of partying. Near the entrance, a lady of the evening approached Skip and said, 'Hey big boy, I can offer you some super sex!'

"Skip thought a moment, then answered, 'I'll take the soup.'"

"Skip has a weight problem. He and his family go to the beach every year during Braves spring training. Last year, his son Josh asked Skip's wife Paula, 'Mom, can I go in the water now?'

"Answered Paula, 'Not now Josh, Daddy is using the ocean.'"

"One day at the ballpark, Skip told me that he was feeling great. 'I feel fit as a fiddle,' he said. I replied, 'Well, how can you feel like a fiddle when you have the shape of a cello?'"

■ Stan Kasten: "I agree that Skip has a weight problem. The other day he went into a men's store and said to the clerk, 'I'd like to see a swim suit in my size.'

"The clerk laughed and said, 'Wow, so would I!'"

"Skip has never been a snappy dresser, we all know that. Last summer, for example, he had this pair of black and white shoes and he wore them every day, until he lost the black one . . ."

■ Pete Van Wieren, Braves announcer: "When Skip's first son, Chip, was born, Skip went to the hospital and saw the baby, just four hours old.

Skip, in his "Pete Van Wieren wig," gets his turn to do the roasting. (Chris Curle)

"Skip was presented the baby and held him in his arms, a big grin on Daddy Skip's face.

"'Well, he's beautiful. Look at that smile, he looks just like me,' Skip said.

"Said the nurse, 'Mr. Caray, please, you're holding him upside down.'"

■ Bobby Cremins, basketball coach, Georgia Tech: "Paula has been putting up with Skip for a long time. Once I asked Skip why his marriage is so successful. Skip explained that two nights a week, they go out for a romantic dinner, with candles, cocktails, wine, the works, and after dinner, they go wild.

"Paula's night out is Tuesday, Skip's is Friday."

"Skip once asked me why so many people take an instant dislike to him.

"I told him, 'Skip, it just saves time!'"

"At work, Skip thinks he's the top dog, and everyone else is a fire hydrant."

"Yes, Skip has been called cheap, cold, rude, and arrogant, but what does Ted Turner know?"

■　■　■

Then it was Skip's turn. Before he thanked his loved ones and friends, he got off a few zingers of his own on the people who'd come to make fun of him:

"Joe Simpson and his lovely wife Kathy bought their first waterbed last week. Kathy already has named it — Lake Placid."

"Joe once had a pet zebra. He named it 'Spot.'"

"Some people like Stan Kasten, but many don't. I was at a party and saw the Surgeon General of the U.S. offer him a cigarette."

"To Bobby Cremins, foreign currency is anything over a $20 bill."

"I don't want to say Ernie Johnson's old, but when he was born, the Dead Sea was just sick."

"One reason I like Don Farmer is that I never get the feeling that he knows something I don't."

■ ■ ■

See why we get along so well? I've had him fooled all these years.

INDEX